TO

Kayleigh & Taylor

FROM

Grandpa & Grammy

DATE

Easter 2013

Many interesting facts about God's creatures!

Daily Devos for Girls WHO LOVE Pets

The quoted ideas expressed in this book (but not Scripture verses) are not, in all cases, exact quotations, as some have been edited for clarity and brevity. In all cases, the author has attempted to maintain the speaker's original intent. In some cases, quoted material for this book was obtained from secondary sources, primarily print media. While every effort was made to ensure the accuracy of these sources, the accuracy cannot be guaranteed. For additions, deletions, corrections, or clarifications in future editions of this text, please write Freeman-Smith.

Scripture quotations are taken from:

The Holy Bible, King James Version

The Holy Bible, New International Version (NIV) Copyright © 1973, 1978, 1984, by International Bible Society. Used by permission of Zondervan Publishing House. All rights reserved.

The Holy Bible, New King James Version (NKJV) Copyright © 1982 by Thomas Nelson, Inc. Used by permission.

The New American Standard Bible®, (NASB) Copyright © 1960, 1962, 1963, 1968, 1971, 1972, 1973, 1975, 1977, 1995 by The Lockman Foundation. Used by permission.

Holy Bible, New Living Translation, (NLT) copyright © 1996. Used by permission of Tyndale House Publishers, Inc., Wheaton, Illinois 60189. All rights reserved.

The Message (MSG)- This edition issued by contractual arrangement with NavPress, a division of The Navigators, U.S.A. Originally published by NavPress in English as THE MESSAGE: The Bible in Contemporary Language copyright 2002-2003 by Eugene Peterson. All rights reserved.

New Century Version®. (NCV) Copyright © 1987, 1988, 1991 by Word Publishing, a division of Thomas Nelson, Inc. All rights reserved. Used by permission.

The Holy Bible, The Living Bible (TLB), Copyright © 1971 owned by assignment by Illinois Regional Bank N.A. (as trustee). Used by permission of Tyndale House Publishers, Inc., Wheaton, Illinois 60189. All rights reserved.

International Children's Bible®, New Century Version®. (ICB) Copyright © 1986, 1988, 1999 by Tommy Nelson™, a division of Thomas Nelson, Inc. All rights reserved. Used by permission.

The Holman Christian Standard Bible™ (HCSB) Copyright © 1999, 2000, 2001 by Holman Bible Publishers. Used by permission.

Cover Design by Kim Russell / Wahoo Designs
Page Layout by Bart Dawson

ISBN 978-1-60587-331-2

Printed in the United States of America

Daily Devos for Girls WHO LOVE Pets

A MESSAGE TO PARENTS

Perhaps your little girl's bookshelf is already filled with an interesting, spirit-lifting collection of children's books. If so, that means you're a thoughtful parent who understands the importance of reading with your child. And if you treasure the time you spend reading with your daughter, this text can be an extremely important addition to her library.

This book contains 365 brief chapters, one for each day of the year. Each chapter contains an important idea from God's Word and a fun fact about the amazing animals that the Creator has placed on this earth.

If your girl loves animals, she'll undoubtedly find the facts on these pages entertaining and informative. But more importantly, this book provides you with 365 different opportunities to share God's wisdom with your daughter, and that's a very good thing.

If you have been touched by God's love and His grace, then you know the joy that He has brought into your own life. Now it's your turn to share His message with the girl whom He has entrusted to your care. Happy reading! And may God richly bless you and your family now and forever.

AREN'T YOU GLAD
GOD MADE ANIMALS?

"For all the wildlife of the earth, for every bird of the sky, and for every creature that crawls on the earth—everything having the breath of life in it. [I have given] every green plant for food." And it was so. God saw all that He had made, and it was very good.

Genesis 1:30-31 HCSB

God made everything in the whole universe, including every person, every pet, and every animal on earth. The more you learn about God's creation—and the more you learn about the animals that live in it—the more amazed you'll be.

From the mighty blue whale to the tiny hummingbird, every animal declares the glory of God. Every dog and cat, every bird and fish, every wild animal and every household pet should remind us of God's miraculous powers.

Do you have a favorite pet? And, do you enjoy reading about the amazing things that animals can do? If so, you'll enjoy the fun facts in this book. And while you're reading, offer a prayer of thanks to God because He made every animal you'll ever learn about . . . and every other animal, too!

God's Amazing Animals: America's Big Bison

The bison, commonly called a "buffalo" can weigh up to 2,000 pounds.

MAKING BETTER DECISIONS

Don't turn your back on wisdom, for she will protect you. Love her, and she will guard you.

Proverbs 4:6 NLT

As you play the game of life, you've got lots of choices to make. Most of those choices are of the smaller variety—like what to do at a given moment, or what to say, or what to wear, or how to direct your thoughts. But a few of your decisions will be BIG, like choosing to be a Christian. Whatever choices you face—whether they're big, little, or somewhere in between—you can be sure that the quality of those choices will make a huge difference in the quality of your life.

How can you make better decisions? A great place to start is by talking things over with God before you spring into action, not after. While you're at it, you can check things out with your parents— or with other concerned adults, like grandparents or teachers. And, you can learn to listen carefully to your conscience.

Pet Facts: When Dogs Get Hot, They Pant

Dogs don't sweat much—in fact, they only sweat on the bottoms of their feet. The main way dogs get rid of body heat is by panting.

ETERNAL LIFE: GOD'S PRICELESS GIFT

I have written these things to you who believe in the name of the Son of God, so that you may know that you have eternal life.

1 John 5:13 HCSB

Your life here on earth is merely a preparation for a far different life to come: the eternal life that God promises to those who welcome His Son into their hearts.

As a mere mortal, your vision for the future is finite. God's vision is not burdened by such limitations: His plans extend throughout all eternity. Thus, God's plans for you are not limited to the ups and downs of everyday life. Your Heavenly Father has bigger things in mind . . . much bigger things.

Today, you have another chance to play the game of life. As you celebrate the wins and struggle through the losses, remember that God has invited you to accept His abundance not only for today but also for all eternity. So keep things in perspective. Although you will inevitably encounter occasional defeats in this world, you'll have all eternity to celebrate the ultimate victory in the next.

God's Amazing Animals: Alligators Are Really Big

The alligator is the largest reptile in North America. The biggest gators can weigh up to 600 pounds.

CHRISTIANITY HERE AND NOW

Teach me to do Your will, for You are my God. May Your gracious Spirit lead me on level ground.

Psalm 143:10 HCSB

God doesn't want you to be a run-of-the-mill, follow-the-crowd kind of girl. God wants you to be a "new creation" through Him. And that's exactly what you should want for yourself, too.

Nothing is more important than your wholehearted commitment to your Creator and to His only begotten Son. Your faith must never be an afterthought; it must be your ultimate priority, your ultimate possession, and your ultimate passion.

You are the recipient of Christ's love. Accept it enthusiastically and share it passionately. Jesus deserves your extreme enthusiasm; the world deserves it; and you deserve the experience of sharing it.

How often it occurs to me, as it must to you, that it is far easier simply to cooperate with God!

Beth Moore

God's Amazing Animals: The World's Biggest Cat

Cats live all over the world. But the biggest cat lives in Asia. It's the Siberian tiger, and it can grow up to be almost 1,000 pounds.

GOD'S LOVE

For the LORD your God has arrived to live among you. He is a mighty Savior. He will rejoice over you with great gladness. With his love, he will calm all your fears. He will exult over you by singing a happy song.

Zephaniah 3:17 NLT

How big is God's love for you? As long as you're alive, you'll never be able to figure it out because God's love is just too big to understand. But this much we know: God loves you so much that He sent His Son Jesus to come to this earth so you could live forever in heaven.

God's love is bigger and more powerful than anybody can imagine, but His love is very real. So do yourself a favor right now: accept God's love with open arms and welcome His Son Jesus into your heart. When you do, your life will be changed today, tomorrow, and forever.

God is a God of unconditional, unremitting love, a love that corrects and chastens but never ceases.

Kay Arthur

God's Amazing Animals: A Pig's Nose Knows!

A pig uses its snout as a tool for finding food in the ground and for making sense of its surroundings.

YOUR CHOICES MAKE A DIFFERENCE

The thing you should want most is God's kingdom and doing what God wants. Then all these other things you need will be given to you.

Matthew 6:33 NCV

There's really no way to get around it: choices matter. If you make good choices, good things will usually happen to you. And if you make bad choices, bad things will usually happen.

The next time you have an important choice to make, ask yourself this: "Am I doing what God wants me to do?" If you can answer that question with a great big "YES," then go ahead. But if you're not sure if the choice you are about to make is right, slow down. Why? Because choices matter . . . a lot!

So if you want to be a winner, be sure to make winning decisions, starting now and ending never.

Freedom is not the right to do what we want but the power to do what we ought.

Corrie ten Boom

God's Amazing Animals: Tigers Live in Lots of Places

Various kinds of tigers live in India, North Korea, South Korea, and Malaysia.

MAKE TODAY A DAY OF CELEBRATION

Always be full of joy in the Lord. I say it again—rejoice!
Philippians 4:4 NLT

What is the best day to celebrate life? This one! Today and every day should be a time for celebration as we consider all the things that God has done.

What do you expect from the day ahead? Are you expecting God to do wonderful things, or are you living beneath a cloud of worry and doubt?

The familiar words of Psalm 118:24 remind us of a profound yet simple truth: "This is the day which the LORD has made." Our duty, as believers, is to rejoice in God's marvelous creation. For Christians, every day begins and ends with God and His Son. Christ came to this earth to give us abundant life and eternal salvation. We give thanks to our Maker when we treasure each day. So with no further delay, let the celebration begin!

We will never be happy until we make God the source of our fulfillment and the answer to our longings.

Stormie Omartian

God's Amazing Animals: Alligators Live a Long Time

An American alligator can live up to 50 years in the wild and up to 70 years in a zoo.

THE PATH TO MATURITY

When I was a child, I spoke and thought and reasoned as a child does. But when I grew up, I put away childish things.

1 Corinthians 13:11 NLT

If you want to be a winner in the game of life, you need to keep learning and growing. The path to spiritual maturity unfolds day by day. Each day offers the opportunity to worship God, to ignore God, or to rebel against God. When we worship Him with our prayers, our words, our thoughts, and our actions, we are blessed by the richness of our relationship with the Father. But if we ignore God altogether or intentionally rebel against His commandments, we rob ourselves of His blessings.

Today offers yet another opportunity for spiritual growth. If you choose, you can seize that opportunity by obeying God's Word, by seeking His will, and by walking with His Son.

Pet Facts: Spotless Baby Dalmatians

Dalmatians are born without spots. As little puppies, they are pure white; their spots develop as they get bigger.

DON'T BE STUBBORN!

Pride comes before destruction, and an arrogant spirit before a fall.

Proverbs 16:18 HCSB

Since the days of Adam and Eve, human beings have been strong-willed and rebellious. Our rebellion stems, in large part, from an intense desire to do things "our way" instead of "God's way." But when we pridefully choose to forsake God's path for our lives, we do ourselves a sincere injustice . . . and we are penalized because of our stubbornness.

God's Word warns us to be humble, not prideful. God instructs us to be obedient, not rebellious. God wants us to do things His way. When we do, we earn lots of blessings—more blessings than we can count. But when we pridefully rebel against our Creator, we sow the seeds of our own problems and we reap a sad, sparse, bitter harvest. May we sow—and reap—accordingly.

Pet Facts: People Like Ferrets

Ferrets are popular! In fact, one survey found that they are currently the third most popular pet in America.

A FRUITFUL FRIENDSHIP

I am the Vine, you are the branches. When you're joined with me and I with you, the relation intimate and organic, the harvest is sure to be abundant.

John 15:5 MSG

Whether you realize it or not, you already have a relationship with Jesus. Hopefully, it's a close relationship! Why? Because the friendship you form with Jesus will help you every day of your life . . . and beyond!

You can either choose to invite Him into your heart, or you can ignore Him altogether. Welcome Him today—and while you're at it, encourage your friends and family members to do the same. Everyone needs Jesus, and that, of course, includes good girls like you.

I am truly happy with Jesus Christ. I couldn't live without Him. When my life gets beyond the ability to cope, He takes over.

Ruth Bell Graham

God's Amazing Animals: Lions Are Large

A big lion can grow up to be 600 pounds or more. That's a very big cat.

GOD'S GREATEST PROMISE

I assure you: Anyone who believes has eternal life.

John 6:47 HCSB

If you learn to depend upon God's promises, you'll always be a winner. So it's time to remind yourself of a promise that God made a long time ago—the promise that God sent His Son Jesus to save the world and to save you! And when you stop to think about it, there can be no greater promise than that.

No matter where you are, God is with you. God loves you, and He sent His Son so that you can live forever in heaven with your loved ones. WOW! That's the greatest promise in the history of the universe. The End.

God has promised us abundance, peace, and eternal life. These treasures are ours for the asking; all we must do is claim them. One of the great mysteries of life is why on earth do so many of us wait so very long to lay claim to God's gifts?

Marie T. Freeman

Pet Facts: Cat Toes

Cats have five toes on each front paw, but only four toes on each back paw!

EXPECTING GOD'S BLESSINGS

My cup runs over. Surely goodness and mercy shall follow me all the days of my life; and I will dwell in the house of the Lord forever.

Psalm 23:5-6 NKJV

Face facts: Christians have every reason to be optimistic and hopeful about life here on earth and life eternal. Mrs. Charles E. Cowman advised, "Never yield to gloomy anticipation. Place your hope and confidence in God. He has no record of failure."

Sometimes, despite our trust in God, we may fall into the spiritual traps of worry, frustration, anxiety, or sheer exhaustion, and our hearts become heavy. What's needed is plenty of rest, a large dose of perspective, and God's healing touch, but not necessarily in that order.

Today, make this promise to yourself and keep it: vow to be a hope-filled Christian. Think optimistically about your life, your education, your team, your family, and your future. And then, when you've filled your heart with hope, share your optimism with your teammates. They'll be better for it, and so will you.

Pet Facts: Dogs Make Faces, Too!

Dogs have many facial expressions, most of them made with their ears.

IT'S NOT HARD TO BE KIND

Therefore, God's chosen ones, holy and loved, put on heartfelt compassion, kindness, humility, gentleness, and patience.

Colossians 3:12 HCSB

How hard is it to say a kind word? Not very! Yet sometimes we're so busy that we forget to say the very things that might make other people feel better.

We should always try to say nice things to our families and friends. And when we feel like saying something that's not so nice, perhaps we should stop and think before we say it. Kind words help; cruel words hurt. It's as simple as that. And, when we say the right thing at the right time, we give a gift that can change someone's day or someone's life.

When we do little acts of kindness that make life more bearable for someone else, we are walking in love as the Bible commands us.

Barbara Johnson

God's Amazing Animals: Bison Are Fast!

The American bison, commonly called a "buffalo" can reach speeds of 30 miles an hour . . . so don't try to outrun one!

ANSWERED PRAYERS

God answered their prayers because they trusted him.

1 Chronicles 5:20 MSG

God answers our prayers. What God does not do is this: He does not answer our prayers in a time and fashion of our choosing, and He does not always answer our prayers by saying, "Yes." Sometimes our loving Heavenly Father responds to our requests by saying "No," and we must accept His answer, even though we may not understand it.

God answers prayers not according to our wishes but according to His master plan. We cannot know that plan, but we can know the Planner . . . and we must trust His wisdom, His righteousness, and His unending love.

What God gives in answer to our prayers will always be the thing we most urgently need, and it will always be sufficient.

Elisabeth Elliot

Pet Facts: Birds Eat Lots of Food!

To survive, every bird must eat at least half its own weight in food each day.

WINNERS KNOW WHEN TO SAY NO

Wisdom will save you from the ways of wicked men....

Proverbs 2:12 NIV

It happens to all of us at one time or another: a friend asks us to do something that we think is wrong. What should we do? Should we try to please our friend by doing something bad? No way! It's not worth it!

Trying to please our friends is okay. What's not okay is misbehaving in order to do so. Do you have a friend who encourages you to misbehave? Hopefully you don't have any friends like that. But if you do, say "No, NO, NOOOOOO!" And what if your friend threatens to break up the friendship? Let her! Friendships like that just aren't worth it.

You will get untold flak for prioritizing God's revealed and present will for your life over man's . . . but, boy, is it worth it.

Beth Moore

Pet Facts: Cats Are Flexible!

Cats are some of the most flexible pets. They can squeeze in places other pets can't.

DIRECTING YOUR THOUGHTS

Finally brothers, whatever is true, whatever is honorable, whatever is just, whatever is pure, whatever is lovely, whatever is commendable— if there is any moral excellence and if there is any praise—dwell on these things.

Philippians 4:8 HCSB

How will you direct your thoughts today? Will you obey the words of Philippians 4:8 by dwelling upon those things that are honorable, pure, and worthy of praise? Or will you allow your thoughts to be hijacked by the negativity that seems to dominate our troubled world?

Are you fearful, angry, bored, or worried? Are you so preoccupied with the concerns of this day that you fail to thank God for the promise of eternity? Are you confused or pessimistic? If so, God wants to have a little talk with you. He wants to remind you of His infinite love and His boundless grace. As you contemplate these things, and as you give thanks for God's blessings, negativity should no longer dominate your day or your life.

Pet Facts: Armadillo Babies

Armadillos have four babies at a time. That means that armadillo moms must be very busy!

CELEBRATING GOD'S HANDIWORK

Christ is the visible image of the invisible God. He existed before God made anything at all and is supreme over all creation.

Colossians 1:15 NLT

When we consider God's glorious universe, we marvel at the miracle of nature. The smallest seedlings and grandest stars are all part of God's infinite creation. God has placed His handiwork on display for all to see, and if we are wise, we will make time each day to celebrate the world that surrounds us.

Today, pause to consider the majesty of heaven and earth. It is as miraculous as it is beautiful, as incomprehensible as it is breathtaking.

The Psalmist reminds us that the heavens are a declaration of God's glory. May we never cease to praise the Father for a universe that stands as an awesome testimony to His presence and His power.

It is impossible for me to look at the heavens at night without realizing there had to be a Creator.

Ruth Bell Graham

Pet Facts: Snake Babies by the Dozens

A mother garter snake can give birth to 85 babies. Do you wonder how she can possibly name them all?

BEYOND ANGER

Mockers can get a whole town agitated, but those who are wise will calm anger.

Proverbs 29:8 NLT

Your temper is either your master or your servant. Either you control it, or it controls you. And the extent to which you allow anger to rule your life will determine, to a surprising extent, the quality of your relationships with others and your relationship with God.

It's a fact: anger and peace simply cannot coexist in the same mind. So be a girl who obeys God's Word by turning away from anger today and every day. You'll be glad you did, and so will your family and friends.

Life is too short to spend it being angry, bored, or dull.

Barbara Johnson

Pet Facts: Cats Don't Forget Much!

Cats have amazing memories! Cats have better memories than dogs. Experiments concluded that while a dog's memory lasts no more than 5 minutes, a cat's can last as long as 16 hours!

A FUTURE SO BRIGHT . . .

Wisdom is pleasing to you. If you find it, you have hope for the future.

Proverbs 24:14 NCV

Let's talk for a minute about the future . . . your future. How bright do you believe your future to be? Well, if you're a faithful believer, God has plans for you that are so bright that you'd better pack several pairs of sunglasses and a lifetime supply of sun block!

The way that you think about your future will play a powerful role in determining how things turn out (it's called the "self-fulfilling prophecy," and it applies to everybody, including you). So here's another question: Are you expecting a terrific tomorrow, or are you dreading a terrible one? The answer to that question will have a powerful impact on the way tomorrow unfolds.

Today, as you live in the present and look to the future, remember that God has an amazing plan for you. Act—and believe—accordingly. And one more thing: don't forget the sun block.

Pet Facts: Plenty of Parrots!

There are over 300 different kinds of parrots: big ones, little ones, and in-between ones. So if you want a parrot, you'll probably find one that's just right for you.

THE PLAN ACCORDING TO GOD

I will instruct you and show you the way to go; with My eye on you, I will give counsel.

Psalm 32:8 HCSB

Maybe you've heard this old saying: "Look before you leap." Well, that saying may be old, but it still applies to you. Before you jump into something, you should look ahead and plan ahead. Otherwise, you might soon be sorry you jumped!

When you acquire the habit of planning ahead, you'll usually make better choices. So when it comes to the important things in life, make a plan and stick to it. When you do, you'll think about the consequences of your actions before you do something silly . . . or dangerous . . . or both.

It's incredible to realize that what we do each day has meaning in the big picture of God's plan.

Bill Hybels

Pet Facts: Old Goldfish

Certain kinds of goldfish can live up to 40 years. That means somebody has to buy plenty of goldfish food!

FOR GOD SO LOVED THE WORLD

This is how much God loved the world: He gave his Son, his one and only Son. And this is why: so that no one need be destroyed; by believing in him anyone can have a whole and lasting life.

John 3:16 MSG

For Christians, death is not an ending; it is a beginning: For believers, the grave is not a final resting-place, it is a place of transition. For Christians, death is not a dark journey into nothingness; it is a homecoming.

God sent His Son as a sacrifice for our sins. Through Jesus, we are redeemed. By welcoming Christ into our hearts, we have received the precious, unfathomable gift of eternal life. Let us praise God for His Son. The One from Galilee has saved us from our sins so that we might live courageously, die triumphantly, and live again—eternally.

Pet Facts: Loveable Labs

In 48 of America's 50 largest cities, the labrador retriever is the most popular breed. But, in Detroit and Miami the German shepherd is the most popular canine pet.

TRUSTING THE QUIET VOICE

In quietness and trust is your strength.

Isaiah 30:15 NASB

Whenever you're about to make an important decision, you should listen carefully to the quiet voice inside. Sometimes, of course, it's tempting to do otherwise. From time to time you'll be tempted to abandon your better judgment by ignoring your conscience. Don't do it!

Instead of ignoring that quiet little voice, pay careful attention to it. If you do, your conscience will lead you in the right direction—in fact, it's trying to lead you right now. So listen . . . and learn.

God desires that we become spiritually healthy enough through faith to have a conscience that rightly interprets the work of the Holy Spirit.

Beth Moore

Pet Facts: All Over the World, People Like Cats

Cats may be more popular than dogs. There are thought to be over 500 million domestic cats in the world.

GOD SOLVES PROBLEMS

Since God assured us, "I'll never let you down, never walk off and leave you," we can boldly quote, God is there, ready to help; I'm fearless no matter what. Who or what can get to me?

Hebrews 13:5-6 MSG

Do you have a problem that you haven't been able to solve? Welcome to the club! Life is full of problems that don't have easy solutions. But if you have a problem that you can't solve, there is something you can do: turn that problem over to God. He can handle it.

God has a way of solving our problems if we let Him; our job is to let Him. God can handle things that we can't. And the sooner we turn our concerns over to Him, the sooner He will go to work solving those troubles that are simply too big for us to handle.

If you're worried or discouraged, pray about it. And ask your parents and friends to pray about it, too. And then stop worrying because no problem is too big for God; not even yours.

Pet Facts: Can You Hold Your Breath Longer Than an Iguana?

Iguanas are able to hold their breath for up to 30 minutes.

LOVE THAT LASTS

It is good and pleasant when God's people live together in peace!

Psalm 133:1 NCV

Are your friends kind to you? And are your friends nice to other people, too? If so, congratulations! If not, it's probably time to start looking for a few new friends. After all, it's really not very much fun to be around people who aren't nice to everybody.

The Bible teaches that a pure heart is a wonderful blessing. It's up to each of us to fill our hearts with love for God, love for Jesus, and love for all people. When we do, we feel better about ourselves.

Do you want to be the best person you can be? Then invite the love of Christ into your heart and share His love with your family and friends. And remember that lasting love always comes from a pure heart . . . like yours!

The attitude of kindness is everyday stuff like a great pair of sneakers. Not frilly. Not fancy. Just plain and comfortable.

Barbara Johnson

Pet Facts: What Do You Call a Group of Puppies?

A group of puppies is called a litter.

HIS LOVE LASTS FOREVER

I am the good shepherd. The good shepherd lays down his life for the sheep.

John 10:11 HCSB

Have you heard the song "Jesus Loves Me"? Of course you have. It's a happy song that should remind you of this important fact: Jesus loves you very much.

When you invite Jesus into your heart, He will be your friend forever. If you make mistakes, He'll still be your friend. When you aren't perfect, He'll still love you. If you feel sorry or sad, He can help you feel better.

Yes, Jesus loves you . . . and you should love yourself. So the next time you feel sad about yourself . . . or something that you've done . . . remember that Jesus loves you, your family loves you, and you should feel that way, too.

He created us because He delights in us!

Beth Moore

Pet Facts: So Many Cats!

There are almost 80 million cats in the United States.

SPIRITUAL WEALTH

Trust in your money and down you go! But the godly flourish like leaves in spring.

Proverbs 11:28 NLT

Sometimes it's hard being a Christian, especially when the world keeps pumping out messages that are contrary to your faith.

The media is working around the clock in an attempt to rearrange your priorities. The media says that your appearance is all-important, that your clothes are all-important, that money is all-important. But guess what? Those messages are lies. The "all-important" things in your life have little to do with stuff. The all-important things in life have to do with your faith, your family, and your future. Period.

Are you willing to stand up for your faith? Are you willing to stand up and be counted, not just in church, where it's relatively easy to be a Christian, but also out there in the "real" world, where it's hard? Hopefully so, because you owe it to God and you owe it to yourself.

Pet Facts: Old Birds

Some birds, like parrots and macaws, can live much longer than dogs or cats—some birds can live up to 75 years!

LAUGHING WITH LIFE

A happy heart makes the face cheerful, but heartache crushes the spirit.

Proverbs 15:13 NIV

Laughter is medicine for the soul, but sometimes, we forget to take our medicine. And that's too bad.

The next time you find yourself dwelling upon the negatives of life, refocus your attention to things positive. The next time you're feeling down, stop yourself and turn your thoughts around. And, if you see your glass as "half empty," you can be sure that your spiritual vision is impaired. With God, your glass is never half empty. With God, your glass is filled to the brim and overflowing . . . forever.

Today, as you go about your daily activities, approach life with a smile on your lips and hope in your heart. And laugh every chance you get. After all, God created laughter for a reason . . . and Father indeed knows best. So laugh!

Pet Facts: Dogs Will Eat Almost Anything!

Dogs eat meat, grains, vegetables, and just about any kind of food you can name.

YOUR ONE-OF-A-KIND FAMILY

Love must be without hypocrisy. Detest evil; cling to what is good. Show family affection to one another with brotherly love. Outdo one another in showing honor.

Romans 12:9–10 HCSB

Your family is a wonderful, one-of-a-kind gift from God. And your family members love you very much—what a blessing it is to be loved!

Have you ever really stopped to think about how much you are loved? Your parents love you (of course) and so does everybody else in your family. But it doesn't stop there. You're also an important part of God's family . . . and He loves you more than you can imagine.

What should you do about all the love that comes your way? You should accept it; you should be thankful for it; and you should share it . . . starting now!

God's Amazing Animals: Tiger Facts

A group of tigers is known as an "ambush" or "streak." And, tigers are good swimmers; they can swim up to three or four miles.

LEARN FROM ANTS

Go to the ant, you slacker! Observe its ways and become wise. Without leader, administrator, or ruler, it prepares its provisions in summer; it gathers its food during harvest. How long will you stay in bed, you slacker? When will you get up from your sleep?

Proverbs 6:6-9 HCSB

The Bible instructs us that we can learn an important lesson from a surprising source: ants. Ants are among nature's most industrious creatures. They do their work without supervision and without hesitation. We should do likewise.

God's Word is clear: We are instructed to work diligently and faithfully. We are told that the fields are ripe for the harvest, that the workers are few, and that the importance of our work is profound. Let us work hard for our Master without hesitation and without complaint. Nighttime is coming. Until it does, let us honor our Heavenly Father with grateful hearts and willing hands.

God's Amazing Animals: Amazing Ants

There are more than 10,000 different kinds of ants. And, bug experts keep discovering new kinds of ants every year.

WHATEVER IT IS, GOD IS BIGGER

Jesus turned around and said to her, "Daughter, be encouraged! Your faith has made you well." And the woman was healed at that moment.

Matthew 9:22 NLT

How can you strengthen your faith? Through praise, through worship, through Bible study, and through prayer. And, as your faith becomes stronger, you will find ways to share it with your friends, your family, and with the world. When you place your faith, your trust, indeed your life in the hands of Christ Jesus, you'll be amazed at the marvelous things He can do with you and through you; so trust God's plans. With Him, all things are possible, and whatever "it" is, God is bigger.

No giant will ever be a match for a big God with a little rock.

Beth Moore

God's Amazing Animals: How Frogs Grow Up

Frogs lay their eggs in water. Then, the eggs hatch into tadpoles which live in water until they grow up and become adult frogs.

TODAY IS YOUR CLASSROOM

If you teach the wise, they will get knowledge.

Proverbs 21:11 NCV

In the game of life, there's always something new to learn. Today is your classroom: what will you learn? Will you be a girl who uses today's experiences as tools for personal growth, or will you ignore the lessons that life and God are trying to teach you? Will you carefully study God's Word, and will you apply His teachings to the experiences of everyday life?

The events of today have much to teach. You have much to learn. May you live—and learn—accordingly.

God's plan for our guidance is for us to grow gradually in wisdom before we get to the crossroads.

Bill Hybels

God's Amazing Animals:
Killer Whales Aren't Really Whales at All!

Killer whales actually belong to the family of oceanic dolphins. That means that killer whales aren't really whales at all.

SHARE YOUR BLESSINGS

Remember this: the person who sows sparingly will also reap sparingly, and the person who sows generously will also reap generously.

2 Corinthians 9:6 HCSB

Jesus told us that we should be generous with other people, but sometimes we don't feel much like sharing. Instead of sharing the things that we have, we want to keep them all to ourselves. But God doesn't want selfishness to rule our hearts; He wants us to be generous.

Are you a girl who is lucky enough to have nice things? If so, God's instructions are clear: you must share your blessings with others. And that's exactly the way it should be. After all, think how generous God has been with you.

It is the duty of every Christian to be Christ to his neighbor.

Martin Luther

God's Amazing Animals:
Gorillas Are Getting Very Hard to Find

Experts currently believe that there are only about 700 mountain gorillas living in the wild. They live high in the mountains in two protected parks in Africa. Lowland gorillas live in central Africa.

SHARING AND SELF-ESTEEM

God loves the person who gives happily.

2 Corinthians 9:7 ICB

Learning how to share can be an important way to build better self-esteem. Why? Because when you learn to share your things, you'll know that you've done exactly what God wants you to do—and you'll feel better about yourself.

The Bible teaches that it's better to be generous than selfish. But sometimes, you won't feel like sharing your things, and you'll be tempted to keep everything for yourself. When you're feeling a little bit stingy, remember this: God wants you to share your things with people who need your help.

When you learn to be a more generous person, God will be pleased with you . . . and you'll be pleased with yourself.

Nothing is really ours until we share it.

C. S. Lewis

God's Amazing Animals: More Tigers in Captivity

There are now more tigers kept in zoos or held privately as pets than there are tigers still living in the wild.

MISTAKES: WE ALL MAKE THEM

LORD, help! they cried in their trouble, and he saved them from their distress.

Psalm 107:13 NLT

Mistakes: nobody likes 'em but everybody makes 'em. In fact, the more you play the game of life, the more mistakes you're bound to make. So even if you're a very good person, you're going to mess things up occasionally. And when you do, God is always ready to forgive you—He'll do His part, but you should be willing to do your part, too.

If you've been engaging in behavior that is against the will of God, cease and desist (that means stop). If you made a mistake, learn from it and don't repeat it (that's called getting smarter). And if you've hurt somebody, apologize and ask for forgiveness (that's called doing the right thing).

Mistakes are the price you pay for being human; repeated mistakes are the price you pay for being stubborn. So don't be hardheaded: learn from your experiences—the first time!

God's Amazing Animals: What to Call a Dolphin

Girl dolphins are called cows, boy dolphins are called bulls, and very young dolphins are called calves.

GETTING GOD'S WISDOM

Understanding is like a fountain which gives life to those who use it.

Proverbs 16:22 NCV

Wisdom is like a savings account: If you add to it consistently, then eventually you will have accumulated a great sum. The secret to success is consistency.

Do you seek wisdom for yourself and for your family? Then you must keep learning, and you must keep motivating them to do likewise. The ultimate source of wisdom, of course, is the Word of God. When you study God's Word and live according to His commandments, you will accumulate wisdom day by day. And finally, with God's help, you'll have enough wisdom to keep and enough left over to share.

A big difference exists between a head full of knowledge and the words of God literally abiding in us.

Beth Moore

God's Amazing Animals: Giraffes Are Heavy

A male giraffe can weigh over 3,000 pounds. So, don't try to pick one up!

WHITE LIES?

Doing what is right brings freedom to honest people.

Proverbs 11:6 ICB

Sometimes, people convince themselves that it's okay to tell "little white lies." Sometimes people convince themselves that itsy bitsy lies aren't harmful. But there's a problem: little lies have a way of growing into big ones, and once they grow up, they cause lots of problems.

Remember that lies, no matter what size, are not part of God's plan for our lives, so tell the truth about everything. It's the right thing to do, and besides: when you always tell the truth, you don't have to try and remember what you said!

Those who are given to white lies soon become color blind.

Anonymous

God's Amazing Animals: Silverback Gorillas Are Bossy

Adult male gorillas are called silverbacks because of the silver-colored fur growing on their backs. Each gorilla family has a silverback leader who scares away other animals by standing on his back legs and beating on his chest!

DIFFICULT DAYS

We take the good days from God—why not also the bad days?

Job 2:10 MSG

Face it: some days are better than others. But even on the days when you don't feel very good, God never leaves you for even a moment. So if you're a girl in need of assistance, you can always pray to God, knowing that He will listen and help.

If you're feeling unhappy, talk things over with God, and while you're at it, be sure and talk things over with your parents, too. And remember this: the sooner you start talking, the sooner things will get better.

When life is difficult, God wants us to have a faith that trusts and waits.

Kay Arthur

God's Amazing Animals: Two Types of Elephants

There are two kinds of elephants: the Asian elephant and the African elephant.

YOUR TO-DO LIST . . . AND GOD'S

Come near to God, and God will come near to you. You sinners, clean sin out of your lives. You who are trying to follow God and the world at the same time, make your thinking pure.

James 4:8 NCV

When you make God's priorities your priorities, you will receive God's blessings. When you make God a full partner in every aspect of your life, He will lead you along the proper path: His path. When you allow God to reign over your heart, He will honor you with spiritual blessings that are simply too numerous to count. So, as you plan for the day ahead, make God's will your ultimate priority. When you do, every other priority will have a tendency to fall neatly into place.

With God, it's never "Plan B" or "second best." It's always "Plan A." And, if we let Him, He'll make something beautiful of our lives.

Gloria Gaither

God's Amazing Animals: What Do You Call a Baby Whale?

A baby whale is called a calf. Adult whales form groups to look after their calves.

FINDING COMFORT

I was very worried, but you comforted me . . . .

Psalm 94:19 NCV

You simply cannot win them all. So, when you get out there and play the game of life, you're bound to have a few worries. Where is the best place to take your worries? Take them to God. Take your troubles to Him; take your fears to Him; take your doubts to Him; take your weaknesses to Him; take your sorrows to Him . . . and leave them all there. Seek protection from the One who offers you eternal life; build your spiritual house upon the Rock that cannot be moved.

Today is mine. Tomorrow is none of my business. If I peer anxiously into the fog of the future, I will strain my spiritual eyes so that I will not see clearly what is required of me now.

Elisabeth Elliot

God's Amazing Animals:
Hummingbirds Go in Every Direction

Hummingbirds are so agile and have such good control that they can fly up, down, forwards, and even backwards.

GOD CARES

For the Lord your God is the God of gods and Lord of lords, the great, mighty, and awesome God.

Deuteronomy 10:17 HCSB

It's a promise that is made over and over again in the Bible: Whatever "it" is, God can handle it.

Life isn't always easy. Far from it! Sometimes, life can be very, very tough. But even then, even during our darkest moments, we're protected by a loving Heavenly Father. When we're worried, God can reassure us; when we're sad, God can comfort us. When our hearts are broken, God is not just near; He is here. So we must lift our thoughts and prayers to Him. When we do, He will answer our prayers. Why? Because He is our Shepherd, and He has promised to protect us now and forever.

The next time you're disappointed, don't panic. Don't give up. Just be patient and let God remind you He's still in control.

Max Lucado

God's Amazing Animals:
It's a Funny Way to Get Some Sleep!

Horses and cows sleep while standing up.

THE WISDOM OF KINDNESS

Kind people do themselves a favor, but cruel people bring trouble on themselves.

Proverbs 11:17 NCV

If we believe the words of Proverbs 11:17—and we should—then we understand that kindness is its own reward. And, if we are to obey the commandments of our Savior—and we should—we must sow seeds of kindness wherever we go.

Kindness, compassion, and forgiveness are hallmarks of our Christian faith. So today, in honor of the One who first showed compassion for us, let's teach our families and friends the art of kindness through our words and through our deeds. Our loved ones are watching . . . and so is God.

Kindness is the universal language that all people understand.

Jake Gaither

God's Amazing Animals: Hippos Like Water

Hippopotamuses spend a large amount of time in rivers, lakes, and swamps. Spending lots of time in water helps hippopotamuses stay cool.

OBEDIENCE AND PRAISE

Praise the Lord! Happy are those who respect the Lord, who want what he commands.

Psalm 112:1 NCV

Psalm 112 links two powerful principles: obedience and praise. One of the most important ways that we can praise God is by obeying Him. As believers who have been saved by a risen Christ, we must worship our Creator, not only with our prayers and our words, but also with our actions.

Are you grateful for God's glorious gifts? Are you thankful for the treasure of eternal life that is yours through the sacrifice of God's Son Jesus? Of course you are. And one of the very best ways to express your gratitude to God is through obedience to the unchanging commandments of His Holy Word.

When you suffer and lose, that does not mean you are being disobedient to God. In fact, it might mean you're right in the center of His will. The path of obedience is often marked by times of suffering and loss.

Charles Swindoll

God's Amazing Animals: What Are Tusks For?

Elephants use their tusks for digging and for finding food.

THE JOYFUL LIFE

Rejoice in the Lord always. I will say it again: Rejoice!
Philippians 4:4 HCSB

C. S. Lewis once said, "Joy is the serious business of heaven." And he was right! God seriously wants you to be a seriously joyful person.

One way that you can have a more joyful life is by learning how to become a more obedient person. When you do, you'll stay out of trouble, and you'll have lots more time for fun.

So here's a way to be a more joyful, happy person: do the right thing! It's the best way to live.

Joy comes not from what we have but from what we are.

C. H. Spurgeon

God's Amazing Animals: Drinking Can Be Dangerous!

Drinking water is one of the most dangerous things a giraffe does. While getting a drink, a giraffe cannot look out for dangerous animals that might want to attack it.

KNOWING HOW TO SHARE

And God will generously provide all you need. Then you will always have everything you need and plenty left over to share with others.

2 Corinthians 9:8 NLT

Are you one of those girls who is lucky enough to have a closet filled up with stuff? If so, it's probably time to share some of it.

When it's time to clean up your closet and give some things away, don't be upset. Instead of complaining, think about all the people who could enjoy the things that you don't use very much. And while you're at it, think about what Jesus might tell you to do if He were here. Jesus would tell you to share generously and cheerfully. And that's exactly what you should do!

The more we stuff ourselves with material pleasures, the less we seem to appreciate life.

Barbara Johnson

God's Amazing Animals: Gorillas Live a Long Time

A gorilla can live for 40 or 50 years. Wow! That's a long time.

YOUR AMAZING TALENTS!

Now there are different gifts, but the same Spirit. There are different ministries, but the same Lord.

1 Corinthians 12:4-5 HCSB

Face facts: you're a girl with very special talents, talents that have been given to you by God. So here's a question: will you use your talents or not? God wants you to use your talents to become a better person and a better Christian. And that's what you should want for yourself.

As you're trying to figure out exactly what you're good at, be sure and talk about it with your parents. They can help you decide how best to use and improve the gifts God has given you.

God has given you special talents—now it's your turn to give them back to God.

Marie T. Freeman

God's Amazing Animals: What Do Butterflies Eat?

Most butterflies feed on nectar from flowers. And by the way, butterflies' taste receptors are on their feet.

WHEN YOU DO THE RIGHT THING

His master said to him, "Well done, good and faithful slave! You were faithful over a few things; I will put you in charge of many things. Enter your master's joy!"

Matthew 25:21 HCSB

God has promised us this: when we do our duties in small matters, He will give us additional responsibilities. When we do our work dutifully, and when we behave responsibly, God rewards us—in a time and in a manner of His choosing, not our own.

Sometimes, God rewards us by giving us additional burdens to bear, or by changing the course of our lives so that we may better serve Him. Sometimes, our rewards come in the form of temporary setbacks that lead, in turn, to greater victories. Sometimes, God rewards us by answering "no" to our prayers so that He can say "yes" to a far grander request that we, with our limited understanding, would never have thought to ask for.

God's Amazing Animals: Ponies May Be Little, but They're Strong!

Pound for pound, ponies are stronger than horses!

GOD IS FAITHFUL

I have set the Lord always before me; because He is at my right hand I shall not be moved.

Psalm 16:8 NKJV

God is faithful. He keeps His promises to us even when we stray far from His will. He continues to love us even when we disobey His commandments. But God does not force His blessings upon us. If we are to experience His love and His grace, we must claim them for ourselves.

Are you discouraged or fearful? Be comforted: God is with you. Are you confused? Listen to the quiet voice of your Heavenly Father. Are you angry? Talk with God and seek His guidance. Are you celebrating a great victory? Thank God and praise Him. He is the Giver of all things good.

In whatever condition you find yourself, wherever you are, whether you are happy or sad, victorious or vanquished, troubled or triumphant, remember that God is faithful and that His love is eternal. And be comforted. God is not just near. He is here.

Pet Facts: So Many Different Kinds of Parrots!

There are about 375 different kinds of parrots. Wow! That's a lot of parrots!

GOD DECIDES

People may make plans in their minds, but the Lord decides what they will do.

Proverbs 16:9 NCV

We win some, and we lose some. So sometimes we must accept life on its terms, not our own. Life has a way of unfolding, not as we will, but as it will. And sometimes, there is precious little we can do to change things.

When events transpire that are beyond our control, we have a choice: we can either learn the art of acceptance, or we can make ourselves miserable as we struggle to change the unchangeable.

We must entrust the things we cannot change to God. Once we have done so, we can prayerfully and faithfully tackle the important work that He has placed before us: the things we can change.

When there is a matter that requires definite prayer, pray until you believe God and until you can thank Him for His answer.

Hannah Whitall Smith

God's Amazing Animals: Polar Bears Are Big

Polar bears aren't just the biggest bears around, they are also the largest meat-eating animals that live on land.

LEARN HOW TO FORGIVE

The discretion of a man makes him slow to anger, and his glory is to overlook a transgression.

Proverbs 19:11 NCV

Bitterness is a form of self-punishment; for-giveness is a means of self-liberation. Bit-terness focuses on the injustices of the past; forgiveness focuses on the blessings of the present and the opportunities of the future. Bitterness is an emotion that hurts you; forgiveness is a decision that empowers you. Bitterness is foolishness; forgive-ness is wisdom.

When we make God's priorities our priorities, He will lead us according to His plan and according to His commandments. When we study God's Word, we are reminded that God's reality is the ultimate re-ality. May we live—and forgive—accordingly.

If Jesus forgave those who nailed Him to the Cross, and if God forgives you and me, how can you withhold your forgiveness from someone else?

Anne Graham Lotz

God's Amazing Animals: Hippos Live a Long Time

A typical hippopotamus can live to be 40 or 50 years old!

WHO SHOULD YOU PLEASE?

A tranquil heart is life to the body, but jealousy is rottenness to the bones.

Proverbs 14:30 HCSB

Sometimes, it's very tempting to be a people-pleaser. But usually, it's the wrong thing to do.

When you worry too much about pleasing friends, you may not worry enough about pleasing God—and when you fail to please God, you inevitably pay a very high price for your mistaken priorities.

Whom will you try to please today: God or your friends? Your obligation is most certainly not to your peers. Your obligation is to an all-knowing and perfect God. Trust Him always. Love Him always. Praise Him always. And seek to please Him and only Him. Always.

We, as God's people, are not only to stay far away from sin and sinners who would entice us, but we are to be so like our God that we mourn over sin.

Kay Arthur

God's Amazing Animals: Plenty of Pigs

Experts estimate that there are about 2 billion pigs in the world.

KEEP YOUR EYE UPON THE DONUT

I am able to do all things through Him who strengthens me.

Philippians 4:13 HCSB

Here's a poem that was seen many years ago in a small donut shop:

> As you travel through life brother,
> Whatever be your goal,
> Keep your eye upon the donut,
> And not upon the hole.

This little poem can remind you of an important lesson: You should spend more time looking at the things you have, not worrying about the things you don't have.

When you think about it, you've got more blessings than you can count. So make it a habit to thank God for the gifts He's given you, and don't feel jealous, angry, or sad about all the other stuff.

God's Amazing Animals:
How Do Polar Bears Stay Warm?

Polar bears keep warm thanks to nearly four inches of blubber (also known as fat) under their skin. They also have very efficient fur, which helps out on those cold winter nights.

WALKING WITH THE WISE

Whoever walks with the wise will become wise; whoever walks with fools will suffer harm.

Proverbs 13:20 NLT

D o you wish to become a wise young woman? Then you must walk with people who, by their words and their presence, make you wiser. And, you must try to avoid people who encourage you to think foolish thoughts or do foolish things.

Today, as a gift to yourself, select, from your friends and family members, a mentor whose judgment you trust. Then listen carefully to your mentor's advice and be willing to accept that advice, even if accepting it requires effort, or pain, or both. Consider your mentor to be God's gift to you. Thank God for that gift, and use it.

Wisdom is knowledge applied. Head knowledge is useless on the battlefield. Knowledge stamped on the heart makes one wise.

Beth Moore

God's Amazing Animals: Too Many Different Kinds of Butterflies to Count!

Scientists believe that there are between 15,000 and 20,000 different kinds of butterflies.

DAILY DISTRACTIONS

If you decide for God, living a life of God-worship, it follows that you don't fuss about what's on the table at mealtimes or whether the clothes in your closet are in fashion. There is far more to your life than the food you put in your stomach, more to your outer appearance than the clothes you hang on your body.

Matthew 6:25 MSG

All of us must live through those days when the traffic jams, the computer crashes, and the dog makes a main course out of our homework. But, when we find ourselves distracted by the minor frustrations of life, we must catch ourselves, take a deep breath, and lift our thoughts upward.

Although we may, at times, struggle mightily to rise above the distractions of everyday living, we need never struggle alone. God is here—eternal and faithful, with infinite patience and love—and, if we reach out to Him, He will restore our sense of perspective and give peace to our souls.

God's Amazing Animals: Elephants Live in Herds

Female elephants spend their entire lives living in large groups called herds. Male elephants leave their herds when they become teenagers and then live mostly by themselves for the rest of their lives.

THE POSSESSIONS WE OWN

We brought nothing into the world, so we can take nothing out. But, if we have food and clothes, we will be satisfied with that.

1 Timothy 6:7-8 NCV

How important is your stuff? Not as important as you might think. In the life of a committed Christian, material possessions should play a rather small role. In fact, when we become overly enamored with the things we own, we needlessly distance ourselves from the peace that God offers to those who place Him at the center of their lives.

Of course, we all need the basic necessities of life, but once we meet those needs for ourselves and for our families, the piling up of possessions creates more problems than it solves. Our real riches, of course, are not of this world. We are never really rich until we are rich in spirit.

Are you one of those girls who is wrapped up in the concerns of the material world? If so, it's time to reorder your priorities by turning your thoughts and your prayers to more important matters. And, it's time to begin storing up riches that will endure throughout eternity: the spiritual kind.

God's Amazing Animals: What Do You Call a Rabbit?

A girl rabbit is called a doe. A boy rabbit is called a buck. And, a baby rabbit is called a kit.

WHEN GOD SPEAKS QUIETLY

Speak, Lord. I am your servant and I am listening.

1 Samuel 3:10 NCV

Sometimes God speaks loudly and clearly. More often, He speaks in a quiet voice—and if you are wise, you will be listening carefully when He does. To do so, you must carve out quiet moments each day to study His Word and sense His direction.

Can you quiet yourself long enough to listen to your conscience? And are you willing to pray sincerely and then to wait quietly for God's response. Hopefully so. Usually God refrains from sending His messages on stone tablets or city billboards. More often, He communicates in quieter ways. If you really desire to hear His voice, you must listen carefully, and you must do so in the silent corners of your quiet, willing heart.

It is in that stillness that the Voice will be heard, the only voice in all the universe that speaks peace to the deepest part of us.

Elisabeth Elliot

God's Amazing Animals: Polar Bears Smell Well

Polar bears have an excellent sense of smell. In fact, they can smell things up to a mile away!

THINK BEFORE YOU SPEAK

To everything there is a season . . . a time to keep silence, and a time to speak.

Ecclesiastes 3:1,7 KJV

Sometimes, it's easier to say the wrong thing than it is to say the right thing—especially if we're in a hurry to blurt out the first words that come into our heads. But, if we are patient and if we choose our words carefully, we can help other people feel better, and that's exactly what God wants us to do.

The Book of Proverbs tells us that the right words, spoken at the right time, can be wonderful gifts to our families and to our friends. That's why we should think about the things that we say before we say them, not after. When we do, our words make the world a better place, and that's exactly what God wants!

The things that we feel most deeply we ought to learn to be silent about, at least until we have talked them over thoroughly with God.

Elisabeth Elliot

God's Amazing Animals: Smart Little Piggy

Pigs are intelligent animals, so intelligent that some people keep them as pets.

HOPE NOW!

When dreams come true, there is life and joy.

Proverbs 13:12 NLT

The hope that the world offers is fleeting and imperfect. The hope that God offers is unchanging, unshakable, and unending.

Where will you place your hopes today? Will you entrust your future to man or to God? Will you seek solace exclusively from fallible human beings, or will you place your hopes, first and foremost, in the trusting hands of your Creator? The decision is yours, and you must live with the results of the choice you make.

For thoughtful believers, hope begins with God. Period. So today, as you embark upon the next stage of your life's journey, consider the words of the Psalmist: "You are my hope; O Lord GOD, You are my confidence" (71:5 NASB). Then, place your trust in the One who cannot be shaken.

God's Amazing Animals: Cold-Weather Birds That Don't Fly

Penguins are birds that don't fly. While other birds have wings for flying, penguins use their flippers to help them swim in the water.

HE'S NUMBER ONE

Let us fix our eyes on Jesus, the author and perfecter of our faith, who for the joy set before him endured the cross, scorning its shame, and sat down at the right hand of the throne of God.

Hebrews 12:2 NIV

Who is in charge of your heart? Is it God, or is it something else? Have you given Christ your heart, your soul, your talents, your time, and your testimony? Or are you giving Him little more than a few hours each Sunday morning?

In the book of Exodus, God warns that we should place no gods before Him. Yet all too often, we place our Lord in second, third, or fourth place as we worship other things. When we unwittingly place possessions or relationships above our love for the Creator, we create big problems for ourselves.

Does God rule your heart? Make certain that the honest answer to this question is a resounding yes. In the life of every thoughtful believer, God comes first. And that's precisely the place that He deserves in your heart.

God's Amazing Animals: Hippos Are Big!

The hippopotamus is the third-largest land animal (after the elephant and the rhinoceros).

GROWING WITH AND BEYOND OUR TROUBLES

We also have joy with our troubles, because we know that these troubles produce patience. And patience produces character, and character produces hope.

Romans 5:3-4 NCV

The next time Old Man Trouble knocks on your door, remember that he has lessons to teach. So turn away Mr. Trouble as quickly as you can, but as you're doing so, don't forget to learn his lessons. And remember: the trouble with trouble isn't just the trouble it causes; it's also the trouble we cause ourselves if we ignore the things that trouble has to teach. Got that? Then please don't forget it!

Every time you refuse to face up to life and its problems, you weaken your character.

E. Stanley Jones

God's Amazing Animals: South Pole, Yes. North Pole, No!

Penguins do live on the continent of Antarctica, near the South Pole. No penguins live at the North Pole, but polar bears do.

THE FUTILITY OF FOOLISH ARGUMENTS

But stay away from those who have foolish arguments and talk about useless family histories and argue and quarrel about the law. Those things are worth nothing and will not help anyone.

Titus 3:9 NCV

Arguments are seldom won but often lost. When we engage in petty squabbles, our losses usually outpace our gains. When we acquire the unfortunate habit of habitual bickering, we do harm to our friends, to our families, and to ourselves.

Time and again, God's Word warns us that most arguments are a monumental waste of time, of energy, of life. In Titus, we are warned to refrain from "foolish arguments," and with good reason. Such arguments usually do more for the devil than they do for God.

So the next time you're tempted to engage in a silly squabble, whether inside the church or outside it, refrain. When you do, you'll put a smile on God's face, and you'll send the devil packing.

God's Amazing Animals: How Kangaroos Get Around

Kangaroos can hop around quickly on two legs or walk around slowly on all four. Kangaroos can't walk backwards.

BLESSED GENEROSITY

The one who blesses others is abundantly blessed;
those who help others are helped.

Proverbs 11:25 MSG

Jesus said, "It is more blessed to give than to receive." That means that we should be generous with other people—but sometimes we don't feel much like sharing. Instead of sharing the things that we have, we want to keep them all to ourselves. That's when we must remember that God doesn't want selfishness to rule our hearts; He wants us to be generous.

Are you lucky enough to have nice things? If so, God's instructions are clear: you must share your blessings with others. And that's exactly the way it should be. After all, think how generous God has been with you.

All kindness and good deeds, we must keep silent. The result will be an inner reservoir of power.

Catherine Marshall

God's Amazing Animals: Florida Loves Their Gators!

People in Florida must admire their gators. In 1987, Florida made the alligator its official state reptile!

ENCOURAGE EACH OTHER

So encourage each other and give each other strength, just as you are doing now.

1 Thessalonians 5:11 NCV

When other people are sad, what can we do? We can do our best to cheer them up by showing kindness and love.

The Bible tells us that we must care for each other, and when everybody is happy, that's an easy thing to do. But, when people are sad, for whatever reason, it's up to us to speak a kind word or to offer a helping hand.

Do you know someone who is discouraged or sad? If so, perhaps it's time to take matters into your own hands. Think of something you can do to cheer that person up . . . and then do it! You'll make two people happy.

One of the best ways to encourage someone who's hurting is with your ears—by listening.

Barbara Johnson

God's Amazing Animals: Big Bird

The ostrich is the largest bird in the world. It also lays the largest eggs.

LOOKING FOR THE GOOD

Dear friend, do not imitate what is evil, but what is good. The one who does good is of God; the one who does evil has not seen God.

3 John 1:11 HCSB

If you look for the good in other people, you'll probably find it. And, if you look for the good things in life, you'll probably find them, too.

But if you spend your time looking for things that aren't so good, you'll most certainly find plenty of bad things to look at. So what should you do? It's simple: you should look for the good things, of course.

When you start looking for good things, you'll find them everywhere: in church, at school, in your neighborhood, and at home.

So don't waste your time on things that make you feel angry, discouraged, worried, guilty, or afraid. Look, instead, for the good things in life, the things that God wants you to pay attention to. You'll be glad you did . . . and God will be glad, too.

God's Amazing Animals: Some Birds Fly Home

Homing pigeons are bred to find their way home from long distances away and have been used for thousands of years to carry messages.

CHEERFUL CHRISTIANITY

A joyful heart is good medicine, but a broken spirit dries up the bones.

Proverbs 17:22 HCSB

Few things in life are more sad, or, for that matter, more absurd, than a grumpy Christian. Christ promises us lives of abundance and joy, but He does not force His joy upon us. We must claim His joy for ourselves, and when we do, Jesus, in turn, fills our spirits with His power and His love.

How can we receive from Christ the joy that is rightfully ours? By giving Him what is rightfully His: our hearts and our souls.

When we earnestly commit ourselves to the Savior of mankind, when we place Jesus at the center of our lives and trust Him as our personal Savior, He will transform us, not just for today, but for all eternity. Then we, as God's children, can share Christ's joy and His message with a world that needs both.

God's Amazing Animals: About Koalas

Koalas are not bears. They are tree-dwelling animals that live in Australia. They eat eucalyptus leaves and almost nothing else.

REMEMBERING GOD'S LOVE

For the Lord is good, and His love is eternal; His faithfulness endures through all generations.

Psalm 100:5 HCSB

How much does God love you? As long as you're alive, you'll never be able to figure it out because God's love is just too big to comprehend. But this much we know: God loves you so much that He sent His Son Jesus to come to this earth and to die for you! And, when you accepted Jesus into your heart, God gave you a gift that is more precious than gold: the gift of eternal life.

God's love is bigger and more powerful than anybody can imagine, but His love is very real. So do yourself a favor right now: accept God's love with open arms and welcome His Son Jesus into your heart. When you do, your life will be changed today, tomorrow, and forever.

Snuggle in God's arms. When you are hurting, when you feel lonely or left out, let Him cradle you, comfort you, reassure you of His all-sufficient power and love.

Kay Arthur

God's Amazing Animals: Squirrels!

There are about 275 different kinds of squirrels.

THE IMPORTANCE OF WORDS

So then, rid yourselves of all evil, all lying, hypocrisy, jealousy, and evil speech. As newborn babies want milk, you should want the pure and simple teaching. By it you can grow up and be saved.

1 Peter 2:1–2 NCV

How important are the words we speak? More important than we realize. Our words have echoes that extend beyond place or time. If our words are encouraging, we can lift others up; if our words are hurtful, we can hold others back.

Do you seek to be a source of encouragement to others? And, do you seek to be a worthy ambassador for Christ? If so, you must speak words that are worthy of your Savior. So avoid angry outbursts. Refrain from impulsive outpourings. Terminate tantrums. Instead, speak words of encouragement and hope to your family and friends, who, by the way, most certainly need all the hope and encouragement they can find.

God's Amazing Animals:
The Popular Polar Bear Goes to the Olympics!

The polar bear was the mascot for the 1998 Winter Olympics in Calgary, Canada.

WHAT'S REALLY IMPORTANT

A pretentious, showy life is an empty life; a plain and simple life is a full life.

Proverbs 13:7 MSG

Here's something to remember about stuff: It's not that important!

Lots of people are in love with money and the things that money can buy. God is not. God cares about people, not possessions, and so must you.

You should not be too concerned about the clothes you wear, or the things you own. And above all, don't ever let your self-esteem depend upon the things that you (or your parents) own.

The stuff that you own isn't nearly as important as the love that you feel in your heart—love for your family, love for your friends, and love for your Father in heaven.

When we put people before possessions in our hearts, we are sowing seeds of enduring satisfaction.

Beverly LaHaye

God's Amazing Animals: A Tiny Bird That Hums

The bee hummingbird is the world's smallest bird. It's just 2 inches long.

YOUR GOOD DEEDS

Therefore by their fruits you will know them.

Matthew 7:20 NKJV

English clergyman Thomas Fuller observed, "He does not believe who does not live according to his beliefs." These words are most certainly true. We may proclaim our beliefs to our hearts' content, but our proclamations will mean nothing—to others or to ourselves—unless we accompany our words with deeds that match. The sermons that we live are far more compelling than the ones we preach.

Like it or not, your life is an accurate reflection of your creed. If this fact gives you some cause for concern, don't bother talking about the changes that you intend to make—make them. And then, when your good deeds speak for themselves—as they most certainly will—don't interrupt.

God's Amazing Animals: Lots and Lots of Sheep

Experts estimate that there are over 1 billion sheep in the world. China has the largest number of sheep in the world.

LOOK TO THE FUTURE, NOT THE PAST

To You, O my Strength, I will sing praises; for God is my defense, my God of mercy.

Psalm 59:17 NKJV

The old saying is familiar: "Forgive and forget." But when we have been hurt badly, forgiveness is often difficult and forgetting is downright impossible. Since we can't forget yesterday's troubles, we should learn from them. Yesterday has much to teach us about tomorrow. We may learn from the past, but we should never live in the past. God has given each of us a glorious day: this one. And it's up to each of us to use this day as faithful stewards, not as embittered historians.

So if you're trying to forget the past, don't waste your time. Instead, try a different approach: learn to accept the past and live in the present. Then, you can focus your thoughts and your energies, not on the troubles of yesterday, but instead on the profound opportunities that God has placed before you today.

God's Amazing Animals: Pigs Will Eat Just About Anything!

When they're hungry (which is most of the time), pigs eat plants, animals, and just about anything else, for that matter.

STUDYING GOD'S WORD

As newborn babies want milk, you should want the pure and simple teaching. By it you can grow up and be saved.

1 Peter 2:2 NCV

When it comes to your faith, God doesn't intend for you to stand still. He wants you to be a girl who keeps moving and growing. In fact, God's plan for you includes a lifetime of prayer, praise, and spiritual growth.

As a Christian, you should continue to grow in the love and the knowledge of your Savior as long as you live. How? By studying God's Word every day, by obeying His commandments, and by allowing His Son to reign over your heart, that's how.

Are you continually seeking to become a more mature believer? Hopefully so, because that's exactly what you owe to yourself and to God.

God's Amazing Animals: Snow Leopards

Snow leopards live in China and Tibet. Fully grown, they weigh about 160 pounds. And just in case you wondered, they do love the snow!

AMAZING GRACE

Saving is all [God's] idea, and all his work. All we do is trust him enough to let him do it. It's God's idea from start to finish! We don't play the major role. If we did, we'd probably go around bragging that we'd done the whole thing! No, we neither make nor save ourselves. God does both the making and the saving.

Ephesians 2:8-9 MSG

Here's the great news: God's grace is not earned . . . and thank goodness it's not! If God's grace were some sort of reward for good behavior, none of us could earn enough brownie points to win the big prize. But it doesn't work that way. Grace is a free offer from God. By accepting that offer, we transform our lives today and forever.

God's grace is not just any old gift; it's the ultimate gift, and we owe Him our eternal gratitude. Our Heavenly Father is waiting patiently for each of us to accept His Son and receive His grace. Let us accept that gift today so that we might enjoy God's presence now and throughout all eternity.

God's Amazing Animals:
Some Penguins Use Other Penguins as Heaters!

Emperor penguins often huddle together to keep warm in the cold temperatures of Antarctica.

GOD'S GOLDEN RULE

Just as you want others to do for you, do the same for them.

Luke 6:31 HCSB

How should you treat other people? Jesus has the answer to that question. Jesus wants you to treat other people exactly like you want to be treated: with kindness, respect, and courtesy. When you do, you'll make your family and friends happy . . . and that's what God wants.

So if you're wondering how to treat someone else, follow the Golden Rule: treat the other people like you want them to treat you. When you do, you'll be obeying your Father in heaven and you'll be making other folks happy at the same time.

It is my calling to treat every human being with grace and dignity, to treat every person, whether encountered in a palace or a gas station, as a life made in the image of God.

Sheila Walsh

Pet Facts: When Cats Get Hot

Cats don't perspire. Why? Because they can't! Cats don't have sweat glands.

TRUST YOUR HEAVENLY FATHER

If God is for us, who is against us?

Romans 8:31 HCSB

What do you expect from the day ahead? Are you expecting God to do wonderful things, or are you living beneath a cloud of fear and doubt? The familiar words of Psalm 118:24 remind us of a profound yet simple truth: "This is the day which the LORD hath made; we will rejoice and be glad in it" (KJV).

For thoughtful Christians, every day begins and ends with God's Son and God's promises. When we accept Christ into our hearts, God promises us the opportunity for earthly peace and spiritual abundance. But more importantly, God promises us the priceless gift of eternal life.

As we face the inevitable challenges of life-here-on-earth, we must arm ourselves with the promises of God's Holy Word. When we do, we can expect the best, not only for the day ahead, but also for all eternity.

Pet Facts: A Fun Fact About Feathers

A bird's feathers weigh more than its skeleton.

RESPECT FOR OTHERS

Being respected is more important than having great riches.

Proverbs 22:1 ICB

Do you try to have a respectful attitude towards everybody? Hopefully so!

Should you be respectful of adults? Of course. Teachers and coaches? Certainly. Family members? Yes. Friends? Yep, but it doesn't stop there. The Bible teaches us to treat all people with respect.

Respect for others is habit-forming: the more you do it, the easier it becomes. So start practicing right now. Say lots of kind words and do lots of kind things, because when it comes to kindness and respect, practice makes perfect.

Don't be a half-Christian. There are too many of them in the world already. The world has a profound respect for a person who is sincere in his faith.

Billy Graham

God's Amazing Animals: Sheep Don't Eat Meat

Sheep are vegetarians, which means that they only eat plants (mostly grass).

PATIENCE AND TRUST

Trust in him at all times, O people; pour out your hearts to him, for God is our refuge.

Psalm 62:8 NIV

Most of us are impatient for the changes that we so earnestly desire. We want solutions to our problems, and we want them right now! But sometimes, life's greatest challenges defy easy solutions, so we must be patient.

Psalm 37:7 commands us to "Rest in the Lord, and wait patiently for Him" (NKJV). But for most of us, waiting quietly for God is difficult. Why? Because we are imperfect beings who seek solutions to our problems today, if not sooner. We seek to manage our lives according to our own timetables, not God's. To do so is a mistake. Instead of impatiently tapping our fingers, we should fold our fingers and pray. When we do, our Heavenly Father will reward us in His own miraculous way and in His own perfect time.

God gave everyone patience—wise people use it.

Anonymous

Pet Facts: The Most Common Bird

The chicken is the most common bird on planet earth.

HIS PROMISES NEVER FAIL

Patient endurance is what you need now, so you will continue to do God's will. Then you will receive all that he has promised.

Hebrews 10:36 NLT

God has made plenty of promises to you, and He will most certainly keep them all. You can find these promises in the book God wrote. It's called the Bible, and you probably already own at least one or two copies. But it's not enough to own Bibles, you should also study.

The Bible is your guide for life here on earth and for life eternal—as a believer, you are called upon to trust its promises, to follow its commandments, and to share its Good News—beginning now and ending never.

Brother, is your faith looking upward today? Trust in the promise of the Savior. / Sister, is the light shining bright on your way? Trust in the promise of thy Lord.

Fanny Crosby

Pet Facts: What Dogs See

Dogs aren't color blind, but they don't see the same colors you do. Dogs see shades of blue, yellow, green and gray, but to a dog, the color red looks gray.

THE JOY OF SERVING GOD

Enjoy serving the Lord, and he will give you what you want.

Psalm 37:4 NCV

Are you a girl who is excited about serving God? You should be. As a believer living in today's challenging world, you have countless opportunities to honor your Father in heaven by serving Him.

Far too many Christians seem bored with their faith and stressed by their service. Don't allow yourself to become one of them! Serve God with thanksgiving in your heart and praise on your lips. Make your service to Him a time of celebration and thanksgiving. Worship your Creator by working for Him, joyfully, faithfully, and often.

God wants us to serve Him with a willing spirit, one that would choose no other way.

Beth Moore

God's Amazing Animals: Where Do Rabbits Live?

Rabbits live in groups. The European rabbit lives underground, in burrows. A group of burrows is known as a warren. More than half of the world's rabbits live in North America.

THE POWER OF PATIENCE

Patience is better than strength. Controlling your temper is better than capturing a city.

Proverbs 16:32 NCV

Temper tantrums are usually unproductive, unattractive, unforgettable, and unnecessary. Perhaps that's why Proverbs 16:32 states that, "Controlling your temper is better than capturing a city."

If you've allowed anger to become a regular visitor at your house, today you must pray for wisdom, for patience, and for a heart that is so filled with love and forgiveness that it contains no room for bitterness. God will help you terminate your tantrums if you ask Him to. And God can help you perfect your ability to be patient if you ask Him to. So ask Him, and then wait patiently for the ever-more-patient you to arrive.

God's Amazing Animals: About the Giant Panda

The giant panda is native to China. It has a black and white coat that features large black patches around its eyes.

UNRELIABLE THINKING

Do not worry about anything, but pray and ask God for everything you need, always giving thanks.

Philippians 4:6 NCV

Charles Swindoll advises, "When you're on the verge of throwing a pity party thanks to your despairing thoughts, go back to the Word of God." How true. Self-pity is not only an unproductive way to think, it is also an affront to your Father in heaven. God's Word promises that His children can receive abundance, peace, love, and eternal life. These gifts are not earned; they are an outpouring from God, a manifestation of His grace. With these rich blessings, how can we, as believers, feel sorry for ourselves? Self-pity and peace cannot coexist in the same mind. Bitterness and joy cannot coexist in the same heart. Thanksgiving and despair are mutually exclusive. So, if your unreliable thoughts are allowing pain and worry to dominate your life, you must train yourself to think less about your troubles and more about God's blessings. When you stop to think about it, hasn't He given you enough blessings to occupy your thoughts all day, every day, from now on? Of course He has! So focus your mind on Him, and let your worries fend for themselves.

Pet Facts: Hamsters Blink, But Not Like You!

Some hamsters only blink one eye at a time.

WORDS SPEAK LOUDER

In every way be an example of doing good deeds. When you teach, do it with honesty and seriousness.

Titus 2:7 NCV

Our words speak, but our actions speak much more loudly. And whether we like it or not, all of us are role models. Our friends and family members observe our actions; as followers of Christ, we are obliged to act accordingly.

Corrie ten Boom advised, "Don't worry about what you do not understand. Worry about what you do understand in the Bible but do not live by." And that's sound advice because our families and friends are always watching . . . and so, for that matter, is God.

One of the best ways to witness to family, friends, and neighbors is to let them see the difference Jesus has made in your life.

Anne Graham Lotz

Pet Facts: Fast-Flying Heartbeats

A bird's heart beats 400 times per minute while they are resting.

PRACTICING FORGIVENESS

Smart people know how to hold their tongue; their grandeur is to forgive and forget.

Proverbs 19:11 MSG

Forgiving other people requires practice and lots of it. So when it comes to forgiveness, here's something you should remember: if at first you don't succeed, don't give up!

Are you having trouble forgiving someone (or, for that matter, forgiving yourself for a mistake that you've made)? If so, remember that forgiveness isn't easy, but it isn't impossible. So keep trying until you get it right . . . and if you keep trying, you can be sure that sooner or later, you will find a way to forgive . . . and when you do, you'll be able to get on with your life.

Forgiveness is a stunning principle, your ticket out of hate and fear and chaos.

Barbara Johnson

God's Amazing Animals:
What, Exactly, Are Chipmunks?

Chipmunks are small squirrels with stripes. They have cheek pouches which help them carry food.

NEW LIFE

When we were baptized, we were buried with Christ and shared his death. So, just as Christ was raised from the dead by the wonderful power of the Father, we also can live a new life.

Romans 6:4 NCV

For faithful Christians, every day begins and ends with God and with His Son. Christ came to this earth to give us abundant life and eternal life. Our task is to accept Christ's grace with joy in our hearts as we receive the "new life" that can be ours through Him.

Believers who fashion their days around Jesus are transformed: They see the world differently; they act differently, and they feel differently about themselves and their neighbors.

Thoughtful Christians face the inevitable challenges and disappointments of each day armed with the joy of Christ and the promise of salvation. So whatever this day holds for you, begin it and end it with God as your partner and Christ as your Savior. And throughout the day, give thanks to the One who created you and saved you. God's love for you is infinite. Accept it joyously and be thankful.

Pet Facts: Dogs Can Do More Than Bark

Most dogs can make between five and ten different vocal sounds.

THE POWER OF HOPE

I wait quietly before God, for my hope is in him.

Psalm 62:5 NLT

The self-fulfilling prophecy is alive, well, and living at your house. If you trust God and have faith for the future, your optimistic beliefs will give you direction and motivation. That's one reason that you should never lose hope, but certainly not the only reason. The primary reason that you, as a believer, should never lose hope, is because of God's unfailing promises.

Thoughts are powerful things. Your thoughts have the power to lift you up or to hold you down. When you acquire the habit of hopeful thinking, you will have acquired a powerful tool for improving your life. So if you find yourself falling into the spiritual traps of worry and discouragement, seek the healing touch of Jesus and the encouraging words of fellow Christians. And if you fall into the terrible habit of negative thinking, think again.

God's Amazing Animals: If You Want to Fly, Pack Light

Birds are lighter than they look. In fact, they have hollow bones that help them fly.

PLANNING AND DILIGENCE

The plans of hard-working people earn a profit, but those who act too quickly become poor.

Proverbs 21:5 NCV

Are you willing to plan for the future—and are you willing to work hard to accomplish the plans that you've made? The Book of Proverbs teaches that the plans of hardworking girls (like you) are rewarded.

If you desire to reap a bountiful harvest from life, you must plan for the future while entrusting the final outcome to God. Then, you must do your part to make the future better (by working dutifully), while acknowledging the sovereignty of God's hands over all affairs, including your own.

Are you in a hurry for success to arrive at your doorstep? Don't be. Instead, work carefully, plan thoughtfully, and wait patiently. Remember that you're not the only one working on your behalf: God, too, is at work. And with Him as your partner, your ultimate success is guaranteed.

God's Amazing Animals:
The Panda Diet: Bamboo, Bamboo, and More Bamboo

The diet of a giant panda is made up almost entirely of bamboo. In fact, a typical panda eats about 20 pounds of bamboo each day.

OBEDIENCE AND SERVICE

When all has been heard, the conclusion of the matter is: fear God and keep His commands.

Ecclesiastes 12:13 HCSB

As you seek to discover God's purpose for your life, you may rest assured that His plan for you is centered around service to your family, to your friends, to your church, to your community, and to the world. God intends that you work diligently on His behalf to serve His children and to share His Good News.

Whom will you choose to serve today? The needs are great and the workers are few. And God is doing His very best to enlist able-bodied believers—like you.

If you want to discover your spiritual gifts, start obeying God. As you serve Him, you will find that He has given you the gifts that are necessary to follow through in obedience.

Anne Graham Lotz

God's Amazing Animals: How Frogs Breathe

Frogs breathe through their noses, but they also take in about half the air they need through their skin.

GOD CAN HANDLE IT

Now the God of all grace, who called you to His eternal glory in Christ Jesus, will personally restore, establish, strengthen, and support you.

1 Peter 5:10 HCSB

Sometimes the future seems bright, and sometimes it does not. Yet even when we cannot see the possibilities of tomorrow, God can. As believers, our challenge is to trust an uncertain future to an all-powerful God.

When we trust God, we should trust Him without reservation. We should steel ourselves against the inevitable disappointments of the day, secure in the knowledge that our Heavenly Father has a plan for the future that only He can see.

Can you place your future into the hands of a loving and all-knowing God? Can you live amid the uncertainties of today, knowing that God has dominion over all your tomorrows? If you can, you are wise and you are blessed. When you trust God with everything you are and everything you have, He will bless you now and forever.

God's Amazing Animals: Fast Tigers!

Tigers have been known to reach speeds up to 40 miles per hour. That's a very fast cat!

PRACTICAL CHRISTIANITY

Therefore as you have received Christ Jesus the Lord, walk in Him.

Colossians 2:6 HCSB

As Christians, we must do our best to ensure that our actions are accurate reflections of our beliefs. Our theology must be demonstrated, not only by our words but, more importantly, by our actions. In short, we should be practical believers, quick to act whenever we see an opportunity to serve God.

Are you the kind of practical Christian who is willing to dig in and do what needs to be done when it needs to be done? If so, congratulations: God acknowledges your service and blesses it. But if you find yourself more interested in the fine points of theology than in the needs of your neighbors, it's time to rearrange your priorities. God needs believers who are willing to roll up their sleeves and go to work for Him. Count yourself among that number. Theology is a good thing unless it interferes with God's work. And it's up to you to make certain that your theology doesn't.

God's Amazing Animals: Sheep Like Company

Sheep like to stay close to each other, which makes it easy for herders to move them around in groups.

OUR INTENTIONS ARE IMPORTANT TO GOD

We justify our actions by appearances; God examines our motives.

Proverbs 21:2 MSG

Other people see you from the outside, and sometimes they judge you by the way you look. God, on the other hand, sees you from the inside—God sees your heart.

Kindness comes from the heart. So does love, caring, sharing, and obedience. These things are all important to God, far more important, in fact, than the way you appear to your friends and neighbors. So don't worry about looking good to the world. Worry, instead about looking good to God. He knows your heart, and He's far more concerned about your intentions and your motivations than He is about your outward appearance.

God's Amazing Animals: Hippos Are Fast!

Although hippos might look slow and fat, they are surprisingly fast. In fact, they can easily outrun a human. So don't try to race a hippo!

COURAGE FOR TODAY . . . AND FOREVER

Don't be afraid, because I am your God. I will make you strong and will help you; I will support you with my right hand that saves you.

Isaiah 41:10 NCV

Christians have every reason to live coura-geously. After all, the ultimate battle has already been won on the cross at Calvary. But even dedicated followers of Christ may find their courage tested by the inevitable disappointments and fears that visit the lives of believers and non-believers alike.

When you find yourself worried about the chal-lenges of today or the uncertainties of tomorrow, you must ask yourself whether or not you are ready to place your concerns and your life in God's all-powerful, all-knowing, all-loving hands. If the answer to that question is yes—as it should be—then you can draw courage today from the source of strength that never fails: your Heavenly Father.

God's Amazing Animals: Flying Squirrels Don't Really Fly

Flying squirrels can't fly like birds, but they do glide between trees. These amazing animals glide the distance of a football field!

TIME FOR GOD

Anyone who comes to him [God] must believe that he exists and that he rewards those who earnestly seek him.

Hebrews 11:6 NIV

When it comes to spending time with God, are you a "squeezer" or a "pleaser"? Do you squeeze God into your schedule with a prayer before mealtime, or do you please God by talking to Him far more often than that? If you're wise, you'll form the habit of spending time with God every day.

Even if you're the busiest girl on Planet Earth, you can still carve out a little time for God. And when you think about it, isn't that the very least you should do?

Have you prayed about your resources lately? Find out how God wants you to use your time and your money. No matter what it costs, forsake all that is not of God.

Kay Arthur

God's Amazing Animals: Dolphins Like Schools

Dolphins live in groups which are called "schools" or "pods." A pod can consist of up to a dozen dolphins.

EXPECTING GREAT THINGS

When a believing person prays, great things happen.

James 5:16 NCV

James 5:16 makes a promise that God intends to keep: when you pray earnestly, fervently, and often, great things will happen. Too many people, however, are too timid or too pessimistic to ask God to do big things. Don't count yourself among their number.

God can and will do great things through you if you have the courage to ask Him and the determination to keep asking Him. Honor God by making big requests. But don't expect Him to do all the work. When you do your part, He will do His part. And when He does, expect a miracle . . . a big miracle.

Prayer moves the arm that moves the world.

Annie Armstrong

God's Amazing Animals: What Gorillas Eat

Gorillas eat wild plants and small insects. Adult gorillas can eat up to 60 pounds of food each day.

WASTED WORDS

A useless person causes trouble, and a gossip ruins friendships.

Proverbs 16:28 NCV

Face it: gossip is bad—and the Bible clearly tells us that gossip is wrong.

When we say things that we don't want other people to know we said, we're being somewhat dishonest, but if the things we say aren't true, we're being very dishonest. Either way, we have done something that we may regret later, especially when the other person finds out.

So do yourself a big favor: don't gossip. It's a waste of words, and it's the wrong thing to do. You'll feel better about yourself if you don't gossip (and other people will feel better about you, too). So don't do it!

To belittle is to be little.

Anonymous

God's Amazing Animals: Elephants Can Swim

Elephants are surprisingly good swimmers. They can even use their trunks to breathe like a snorkel in deep water.

LEARNING HOW TO FORGIVE

Above all, keep your love for one another at full strength, since love covers a multitude of sins.

1 Peter 4:8 HCSB

If you want to be a genuine winner in the game of life, you need to learn how to forgive people. Why? Because our loved ones are imperfect (as are we). How often must we forgive our family and friends? More times than we can count. Why? Because that's what God wants us to do.

Perhaps granting forgiveness is hard for you. If so, you are not alone. Genuine, lasting forgiveness is often difficult to achieve—difficult but not impossible. Thankfully, with God's help, all things are possible, and that includes forgiveness. But, even though God is willing to help, He expects you to do some of the work. And make no mistake: forgiveness is work, which is okay with God. He knows that the payoffs are worth the effort.

God's Amazing Animals: Some Turtles Are Very Big!

The largest turtle is the leatherback sea turtle. The largest leatherback turtle ever found weighed 2,020 pounds.

ROOM TO GROW

So let us stop going over the basics of Christianity again and again. Let us go on instead and become mature in our understanding.

Hebrews 6:1 NLT

Are you a fully-grown girl? Physically: maybe you're getting close. But spiritually? No way! And thank goodness that you're not! Even if you're very mature for your age, you've still got lots of room to grow.

The 19th-century writer Hannah Whitall Smith observed, "The maturity of a Christian experience cannot be reached in a moment." No kidding. In truth, the search for spiritual growth lasts a lifetime.

When we cease to grow, either emotionally or spiritually, we do ourselves and our families a profound disservice. But, if we study God's Word, if we obey His commandments, and if we live in the center of His will, we will not be "stagnant" believers; we will, instead, be growing Christians . . . and that's exactly what God wants for our lives. Come to think of it, that's exactly what you should want, too.

God's Amazing Animals: Two Wings . . . and Two More

Butterflies have four wings.

GOD KNOWS BEST

However, each one must live his life in the situation the Lord assigned when God called him.

1 Corinthians 7:17 HCSB

Here are three things to think about: 1. God loves you. 2. God wants what's best for you. 3. God has a plan for you.

God's plan may not always happen exactly like you want, but remember: God always knows best. Sometimes, even though you may want something very badly, you must still be patient and wait for the right time to get it, And the right time, of course, is determined by God.

Even if you don't get exactly what you want today, you can be sure that God wants what's best for you . . . today, tomorrow, and forever.

God has plans—not problems—for our lives.

Corrie ten Boom

God's Amazing Animals: Giraffes Have Heavy Hair!

The hair of a giraffes tail is about 10 times thicker than an average human hair.

SHINING LIKE STARS

The wise people will shine like the brightness of the sky. Those who teach others to live right will shine like stars forever and ever.

Daniel 12:3 NCV

Our world needs Christian leaders who "will shine like stars forever and ever." Our world needs leaders who willingly honor God with their words and their deeds—with the emphasis on deeds.

If you seek to be a godly leader, then you must begin by being a worthy example to your family, to your friends, to your teammates, to your church, and to your community. After all, your words of instruction will never ring true unless you yourself are willing to follow them.

Are you the kind of leader whom you would want to follow? If so, congratulations. But if the answer to that question is no, then it's time to improve your leadership skills, beginning with the words that you speak and the example that you set. And the greatest of these, not surprisingly, is example.

Pet Facts: A Dog's Nose Knows Best

A dog's nose has about 4 times as many scent cells as a cat's nose and 14 times more than a human's nose. That's why dogs are such good sniffers!

SHARE THE GOOD NEWS

Christ did not send me to baptize people but to preach the Good News. And he sent me to preach the Good News without using words of human wisdom so that the cross of Christ would not lose its power.

1 Corinthians 1:17 NCV

A good way to build your faith is by talking about it—and that's precisely what God wants you to do.

In his second letter to Timothy, Paul shares a message to believers of every generation when he writes, "God has not given us a spirit of timidity" (1:7). Paul's meaning is clear: When sharing your testimony, you must be courageous and unashamed.

Let's face facts: You live in a world that desperately needs the healing message of Jesus Christ. Every believer, including you, bears responsibility for sharing the Good News. And it is important to remember that you give your testimony through your words and your actions. And, as the old saying goes, actions speak louder than words.

God's Amazing Animals:
How Long Do Giant Pandas Live?

Giant pandas in the wild usually live to be about 20 years of age.

CONCERNING STUFF

Prosperity is as short-lived as a wildflower, so don't ever count on it.

James 1:10 MSG

Are you a girl who's overly concerned with the stuff that money can buy? Hopefully not. On the grand stage of a well-lived life, material possessions should play a rather small role. Of course, we all need the basic necessities of life, but once we meet those needs for ourselves and for our families, the piling up of possessions creates more problems than it solves. Our real riches, of course, are not of this world. We are never really rich until we are rich in spirit.

Our society is in love with money and the things that money can buy. God is not. God cares about people, not possessions, and so must we. We must, to the best of our abilities, love our neighbors as ourselves, and we must, to the best of our abilities, resist the mighty temptation to place possessions ahead of people.

Money, in and of itself, is not evil; worshipping money is. So today, as you prioritize matters of importance in your life, remember that God is almighty, but the dollar is not.

Pet Facts: Cats Are Terrific Jumpers!

A cat can jump as much as 7 times its height.

WORKING WITH HEART AND SOUL

He was diligent in every deed that he began in the service of God's temple, in the law and in the commandment, in order to seek his God, and he prospered.

2 Chronicles 31:21 HCSB

How does God intend for us to work? Does He intend for us to work diligently or does He, instead, reward mediocrity? The answer is obvious. God has created a world in which hard work is rewarded and sloppy work is not. Yet sometimes, we may seek ease over excellence, or we may be tempted to take shortcuts when God intends that we walk the straight and narrow path.

Today, heed God's Word by doing good work. Wherever you find yourself, whatever your job description, do your work, and do it with all your heart. When you do, you will most certainly win the recognition of your peers. But more importantly, God will bless your efforts and use you in ways that only He can understand. So do your work with focus and dedication. And leave the rest up to God.

Pet Facts: No Chocolate for Your Pets

Chocolate is poisonous to both cats and dogs.

THE POWER OF POSITIVE FRIENDSHIPS

Light shines on those who do right; joy belongs to those who are honest. Rejoice in the Lord, you who do right. Praise his holy name.

Psalm 97:11-12 NCV

If you'd like to build a positive life, find positive friends. If you'd like to live a godly life, seek the fellowship of godly friends. If you'd like to live passionately, prayerfully, and purposefully, spend time with people who are already living passionate, prayerful, purposeful lives. Soon, you'll discover that you will inevitably become more and more like the people who surround you day in and day out.

In choosing your friends, you set your course for the future. So choose carefully . . . very carefully.

The glory of friendship is not the outstretched hand, or the kindly smile, or the joy of companionship. It is the spiritual inspiration that comes to one when he discovers that someone else believes in him and is willing to trust him with his friendship.

Corrie ten Boom

God's Amazing Animals: Want to Win a Race? Race a Turtle!

Turtles are very slow. Carrying around that heavy shell doesn't help!

WHO RULES?

Do not worship any other gods besides me.

Exodus 20:3 NLT

Who rules your heart? Is it God, or is it something else?

In the book of Exodus, God warns that we should place no gods before Him. Yet all too often, we place our Lord in second, third, or fourth place as we worship the gods of pride, greed, power, or personal gratification. When we unwittingly place possessions or relationships above our love for the Creator, we must seek His forgiveness and change our ways.

Does God rule your heart? Make certain that the honest answer to this question is a resounding yes. In the life of every righteous believer, God comes first. And that's precisely the place that He deserves in your heart.

A sense of deity is inscribed on every heart.

John Calvin

Pet Facts: Old Dogs Can Learn, Just Not as Quickly

With patience you can teach any old dog new tricks. Dogs can learn new tricks at any age, but dogs, like people, have a hard time breaking old habits because old habits are hard to break.

STOPPING TO THINK

Knowing God leads to self-control. Self-control leads to patient endurance, and patient endurance leads to godliness.

2 Peter 1:6 NLT

Maybe you're one of those girls who tries to do everything fast, faster, or fastest! If so, maybe you sometimes do things before you think about the consequences of your actions. If that's the case, it's probably a good idea to slow down a little bit so you can think before you act. When you do, you'll soon discover the value of thinking carefully about things before you get started. And while you're at it, it's probably a good idea to think before you speak, too. After all, you'll never have to apologize for something that you didn't say.

If you can't seem to put the brakes on impulsive behavior, you're probably not praying hard enough.

Jim Gallery

Pet Facts: What Do You Call a Cat?

A boy cat is called a tom; a girl cat is called a molly or queen; a baby cat is called a kitten.

THANKING GOD FOR HIS GIFTS

Thanks be to God for his indescribable gift!

2 Corinthians 9:15 NIV

How do we thank God for the gifts He has given us? By using those gifts, that's how!

God has given you talents and opportunities that are uniquely yours. Are you willing to use your gifts in the way that God intends? And are you willing to summon the discipline that is required to develop your talents and to hone your skills? That's precisely what God wants you to do, and that's precisely what you should desire for yourself.

As you seek to expand your talents, you will undoubtedly encounter stumbling blocks along the way, such as the fear of rejection or the fear of failure. When you do, don't stumble! Just continue to refine your skills, and offer your services to God. And when the time is right, He will use you—but it's up to you to be thoroughly prepared when He does.

What we are is God's gift to us. What we become is our gift to God.

Anonymous

God's Amazing Animals: So Many Kinds of Owls!

There are about 200 different kinds of owls.

JESUS CAN TAKE CARE OF OUR PROBLEMS

Do not love the world or the things that belong to the world. If anyone loves the world, love for the Father is not in him.

1 John 2:15 HCSB

An old hymn contains the words, "This world is not my home; I'm just passing through." Thank goodness! This crazy world can be a place of trouble and danger. Thankfully, your real home is heaven, a place where you can live forever with Jesus.

In John 16:33, Jesus tells us He has overcome the troubles of this world. We should trust Him, and we should plan our days and our lives accordingly. When we do, we are forever blessed by the Son of God and His Father in heaven.

If you dwell on the world's message, you're setting yourself up for disaster. If you dwell on God's message, you're setting yourself up for victory.

Jim Gallery

Pet Facts: How Long Do Dogs Live?

The average lifespan for mixed-breed and midsize dogs is about 13 to 14 years.

THE CHEERFUL GIVER

God loves the person who gives cheerfully.

2 Corinthians 9:7 NLT

Are you a cheerful giver? If you intend to obey God's commandments, you must be. When you give, God looks not only at the quality of your gift, but also at the condition of your heart. If you give generously, joyfully, and without complaint, you obey God's Word. But, if you make your gifts grudgingly, or if the motivation for your gift is selfish, you disobey your Creator, even if you have tithed in accordance with Biblical principles.

Today, take God's commandments to heart and make this pledge: Be a cheerful, generous, courageous giver. The world needs your help, and you need the spiritual rewards that will be yours when you give faithfully, prayerfully, and cheerfully.

The test of generosity is not how much you give, but how much you have left.

Anonymous

God's Amazing Animals: Polar Bears Are Heavy

Polar bears can weigh up to 1,500 pounds. That's a very big bear!

GETTING TO KNOW GOD

Stay clear of silly stories that get dressed up as religion. Exercise daily in God—no spiritual flabbiness, please!

1 Timothy 4:7 MSG

Want to know God better? Then schedule a meeting with Him every day.

Each day has 1,440 minutes—will you spend a few of those minutes with your Heavenly Father? He deserves that much of your time and more. God wants you to pay attention to Him. So, if you haven't already done so, form the habit of spending quality time with your Creator. He deserves it . . . and so, for that matter, do you.

We all need to make time for God. Even Jesus made time to be alone with the Father.

Kay Arthur

Pet Facts: Big Dogs, Little Dogs

Dogs vary greatly in size. The smallest breed is the Chihuahua. It weighs only 4 pounds and is 5 inches high at the shoulders. The tallest breed is the Irish wolfhound. It is about 39 inches tall at the shoulders.

LIVING IN THE SPIRIT OF TRUTH

But when the Spirit of truth comes, he will lead you into all truth.

John 16:13 NCV

God is vitally concerned with truth. His Word teaches the truth; His Spirit reveals the truth; His Son leads us to the truth. When we open our hearts to God, and when we allow His Son to rule over our thoughts and our lives, God reveals Himself, and we come to understand the truth about ourselves and the Truth about God's gift of grace.

The familiar words of John 8:32 remind us that "you shall know the truth, and the truth shall make you free" (NKJV). May we, as believers, seek God's truth and live by it, this day and forever.

Those who walk in truth walk in liberty.

Beth Moore

Pet Facts: How Do Cats Play Best?

Cat families usually play best in even numbers. Cats and kittens should be acquired in pairs whenever possible.

THE WISDOM OF THANKSGIVING

Give thanks to the Lord, for He is good; His faithful love endures forever.

Psalm 106:1 HCSB

God's Word makes it clear: a wise heart is a thankful heart. Period. We are to worship God, in part, by the genuine gratitude we feel in our hearts for the marvelous blessings that our Creator has bestowed upon us. Yet even the most saintly among us must endure periods of bitterness, fear, doubt, and regret. Why? Because we are imperfect human beings who are incapable of perfect gratitude. Still, even on life's darker days, we must seek to cleanse our hearts of negative emotions and fill them, instead, with praise, with love, with hope, and with thanksgiving. To do otherwise is to be unfair to ourselves, to our loved ones, and to our God.

God's Amazing Animals:
You Can Tell a Zebra by Its Stripes

No two zebras have stripes that are exactly alike. But it's still hard to tell one zebra from another, unless, of course, you happen to be a zebra!

LEARNING LIFE'S LESSONS . . .
THE EASY WAY

Whoever is stubborn after being corrected many times will suddenly be hurt beyond cure.

Proverbs 29:1 NCV

When it comes to learning life's lessons, we can either do things the easy way or the hard way. The easy way can be summed up as follows: when God teaches us a lesson, we learn it . . . the first time! Unfortunately, too many of us learn much more slowly than that.

When we resist God's instruction, He continues to teach, whether we like it or not. Our challenge, then, is to discern God's lessons from the experiences of everyday life. Hopefully, we learn those lessons sooner rather than later because the sooner we do, the sooner He can move on to the next lesson and the next and the next . . .

God's Amazing Animals: Loud Lions

An adult lion's roar can be heard up to five miles away. That means that if you lived with a pride of lions, you'd probably need ear plugs!

THE POSITIVE PATH

But the path of the just is like the shining sun, that shines ever brighter unto the perfect day. The way of the wicked is like darkness; they do not know what makes them stumble.

Proverbs 4:18-19 NKJV

When Jesus addressed His disciples, He warned that each one must, "take up his cross and follow Me." The disciples must have known exactly what the Master meant. In Jesus' day, prisoners were forced to carry their own crosses to the location where they would be put to death. Thus, Christ's message was clear: in order to follow Him, Christ's disciples must deny themselves and, instead, trust Him completely. Nothing has changed since then.

If we are to be faithful disciples of the One from Galilee, we must trust Him and we must follow Him. Jesus never comes "next." He is always first. He shows us the path of life.

Do you seek to be a worthy disciple of Jesus? Then pick up His cross today and follow in His footsteps. When you do, you can walk with confidence: He will never lead you astray.

God's Amazing Animals: Owls Work the Night Shift

Owls are active at night (nocturnal).

LIFE IS GREAT!

Rejoice in the Lord, you righteous ones; praise from the upright is beautiful.

Psalm 33:1 HCSB

Life should never be taken for granted. Each day is a priceless gift from God and should be treated as such.

Hannah Whitall Smith observed, "How changed our lives would be if we could only fly through the days on wings of surrender and trust!" These words remind us that this day is God's creation, a gift to be treasured and enjoyed . . . starting now.

So if you're waiting for happiness to arrive at your doorstep "some day," wait no more. The best day to rejoice is this one.

The highest and most desirable state of the soul is to praise God in celebration for being alive.

Luci Swindoll

God's Amazing Animals: Polar Bears Move Fast

Polar bears can reach speeds up to 25 miles per hour on land and 6 miles per hour in water.

GOD'S RULE BOOK

Therefore, since we have this ministry, as we have received mercy, we do not give up. Instead, we have renounced shameful secret things, not walking in deceit or distorting God's message, but in God's sight we commend ourselves to every person's conscience by an open display of the truth.

2 Corinthians 4:1-2 HCSB

God has given us a guidebook for righteous living called the Holy Bible. It contains thorough instructions which, if followed, lead to fulfillment, righteousness, and eternal life. But, if we choose to ignore God's commandments, the results are as predictable as they are tragic.

A righteous life has many components: faith, honesty, generosity, love, kindness, humility, gratitude, and worship, to name but a few. If we seek to follow the steps of our Savior, Jesus Christ, we must seek to live according to His commandments. In short, we must, to the best of our abilities, live according to the principles contained in God's Holy Word.

Pet Facts: Yorky Hair

The Yorkshire terrier has hair that can be two feet long, or longer!

SHARE GOD'S LOVE

My dear, dear friends, if God loved us like this, we certainly ought to love each other.

1 John 4:11 MSG

God loves you. How will you respond to His love? The Bible clearly defines what your response should be: "You shall love the Lord your God with all your heart, with all your soul, and with all your strength" (Deuteronomy 6:5 NKJV). But you must not stop there. You must also love your neighbor as yourself. Jesus teaches that "On these two commandments hang all the Law and the Prophets" (Matthew 22:40).

Today, as you meet the demands of everyday living, will you pause long enough to return God's love? And then will you share it? Prayerfully, you will. When you embrace God's love, you are forever changed. When you embrace God's love, you feel differently about yourself, your family, your friends, and your world. When you embrace God's love, you have enough love to keep and enough love to share: enough love for a day, enough love for a lifetime, enough love for all eternity.

God's Amazing Animals: Now That's a Big Tooth!

An elephant's tooth can weigh as much as 12 pounds.

GOD IS LOVE

For God so loved the world that he gave his only Son, so that everyone who believes in him will not perish but have eternal life.

John 3:16 NLT

The Bible makes this promise: God is love. It's a big promise, a very important description of what God is and how God works. God's love is perfect. When we open our hearts to His love, we are blessed and we are protected.

Today, offer sincere prayers of thanksgiving to your Heavenly Father. He loves you now and throughout all eternity. Open your heart to His presence and His love.

No part of our prayers creates a greater feeling of joy than when we praise God for who He is. He is our Master Creator, our Father, our source of all love.

Shirley Dobson

God's Amazing Animals: Whiskers Can Be Very Useful

Cats can use their whiskers to check and see whether a space is too small for them to fit through.

A PERFECT TIMETABLE

He has made everything appropriate in its time. He has also put eternity in their hearts, but man cannot discover the work God has done from beginning to end.

Ecclesiastes 3:11 HCSB

O f this you can be sure: God's sense of timing is without error. God's timing may not coincide with your preferred timing—which, by the way, is perfectly fine with God because He knows precisely what He's doing, even if you may not.

Perhaps you're impatient for God to reveal His plans for your life. If so, it is time to reread the third chapter of Ecclesiastes. Solomon's words will remind you that there is a time for every purpose under God's heaven—and that includes your purpose.

Waiting on God brings us to the journey's end quicker than our feet.

Mrs. Charles E. Cowman

God's Amazing Animals: Mountain Lions Have Uneven Legs!

Mountain lions are strong jumpers, thanks to strong back legs that are longer than their front legs.

WHAT CAN I LEARN TODAY?

It takes knowledge to fill a home with rare and beautiful treasures.

Proverbs 24:4 NCV

If we are to grow as Christians, we need both knowledge and wisdom. Knowledge is found in textbooks and in classrooms. Wisdom, on the other hand, is found in God's Holy Word and in the carefully-chosen words of loving parents, family members, and friends. Knowledge is an important building block in a well-lived life, and it pays rich dividends both personally and professionally. But, wisdom is even more important because it refashions not only the mind, but also the heart.

A big difference exists between a head full of knowledge and the words of God literally abiding in us.

Beth Moore

God's Amazing Animals: Non-Stop Teeth

A rabbit's teeth never stops growing. They are kept worn down by the rabbits gnawing on food.

PATIENCE WITH OTHERS AND ONE'S SELF

God has chosen you and made you his holy people. He loves you. So always do these things: Show mercy to others, be kind, humble, gentle, and patient.

Colossians 3:12 NCV

The dictionary defines the word patience as "the ability to be calm, tolerant, and understanding." If that describes you, you can skip the rest of this page. But, if you're like most of us, you'd better keep reading.

For most of us, patience is a hard thing to master. Why? Because we have lots of things we want, and we want them NOW (if not sooner). But the Bible tells us that we must learn to wait patiently for the things that God has in store for us.

The next time you find your patience tested to the limit, remember that the world unfolds according to God's timetable, not yours. Sometimes, you must wait patiently, and that's as it should be. After all, think how patient God has been with you!

God's Amazing Animals: Cheetahs Can Make Long Jumps!

In a single stride, a cheetah can cover 25 feet. No wonder they're so fast!

YOU'RE SO VERY SPECIAL

Blessed is the man who does not condemn himself.

Romans 14:22 HCSB

When God made you, He made you in a very special way. In fact, you're a wonderful, one-of-a-kind creation, a special person unlike any other.

Do you realize how special you are? Do you know that God loves you because of who you are (not because of the things you've done)? And do you know that God has important work for you to do? Well whether you realize it or not, all these things are true.

So the next time you feel bad about something you've done, take a look in the mirror, and remember that you're looking at a wonderfully special person . . . you!

God loves you . . . and that's the way that you should feel about yourself, too.

God's Amazing Animals: That's Big!

The world's largest animal is the blue whale. Fully grown, it weighs as much as 150 tons and is almost 90 feet long.

HIS PLANS . . . AND YOURS

There is no wisdom, understanding, or advice that can succeed against the Lord.

Proverbs 21:30 NCV

Does God have a game plan for your life? Of course He does! Every day of your life, He is trying to lead you along a path of His choosing . . . but He won't force you to follow. God has given you free will, the opportunity to make decisions for yourself. The choices are yours: either you will choose to obey His Word and seek His will, or you will choose to follow a different path.

God's plans for you may be far bigger than you imagine, but He may be waiting for you to make the next move—so today, make that move prayerfully, faithfully, and expectantly. And after you've made your move, trust God to make His.

The one supreme business of life is to find God's plan for your life and live it.

E. Stanley Jones

Pet Facts: How Many Kinds of Dogs are in America?

The American Kennel Club recognizes 175 different dog breeds.

WISDOM IS AS WISDOM DOES

A foolish person enjoys doing wrong, but a person with understanding enjoys doing what is wise.

Proverbs 10:23 NCV

D o you want to become wise? If so, you must behave wisely. Wisdom is as wisdom does.

High-sounding platitudes are as common as table salt. Aphorisms are everywhere. Parables proliferate. No matter. Wisdom is denominated not by words, but by deeds.

Do you wish to be a young woman who walks among the wise? If so, you must walk wisely. There is simply no other way.

No matter how many books you read, no matter how many schools you attend, you're never really wise until you start making wise choices.

Marie T. Freeman

Pet Facts: How Big Is a Litter of Kittens?

The average litter of kittens is between 2 and 6. Those are "purrrrrrrrr-ty" nice numbers, don't you think?

PARENTS AND COACHES CAN HELP YOU BE SUCCESSFUL

Success, success to you, and success to those who help you, for your God will help you . . . .

1 Chronicles 12:18 NIV

God makes this promise: If you have faith in Him, you can do BIG things! So if you have something important to do, pray about it and ask God for help. When you ask God to help you, He will. And while you're at it, never be afraid to ask your parents for their help, too.

When you talk things over with your parents and coaches, you'll soon discover that they want you to do BIG things . . . and they can give you LOTS of help along the way.

Success and happiness are not destinations. They are exciting, never-ending journeys.

Zig Ziglar

God's Amazing Animals: Half on Land, Half at Sea

Penguins spend about half their time in the water and the other half of their time on land.

ON GUARD AGAINST EVIL

Your love must be real. Hate what is evil, and hold on to what is good.

Romans 12:9 NCV

Face facts: this world is inhabited by quite a few people who are very determined to do evil things. The devil and his human helpers are working 24/7 to cause pain and heartbreak in every corner of the globe . . . including your corner. So you'd better beware.

Your job, if you choose to accept it, is to recognize evil and fight it. The moment that you decide to fight evil whenever you see it, you can no longer be a lukewarm, halfhearted Christian. And, when you are no longer a lukewarm Christian, God rejoices while the devil despairs.

When will you choose to get serious about fighting the evils of our world? Before you answer that question, consider this: in the battle of good versus evil, the devil never takes a day off . . . and neither should you.

God's Amazing Animals:
Bet You Can't Hold Your Breath That Long

Elephant seals are air-breathing mammals, but they can hold their breath for up to two hours while diving. Wow!

ONLY ONE YOU

To acquire wisdom is to love oneself; people who cherish understanding will prosper.

Proverbs 19:8 NLT

Do you really like the person you see when you look into the mirror? You should! After all, the person in the mirror is a very special person who is made—and loved—by God.

In fact, you are loved in many, many ways: God loves you, your parents love you, and your family loves you, for starters. So you should love yourself, too.

So here's something to think about: since God thinks you're special, and since so many people think you're special, isn't it about time for you to agree with them? Of course it is! It's time to say, "You're very wonderful and very special," to the person you see in the mirror.

Even if you don't love yourself, God does. And He's right.

Anonymous

God's Amazing Animals: Got Milk?

Amazingly, a cow gives nearly 200,000 glasses of milk in her lifetime.

BEYOND ANXIETY

Anxiety in a man's heart weighs it down, but a good word cheers it up.

Proverbs 12:25 HCSB

God calls us to live above and beyond our worries. God calls us to live by faith, not by fear. He instructs us to trust Him completely, this day and forever. But sometimes, trusting God is difficult, especially when we become caught up in the incessant demands of an anxious world.

When you feel anxious—and you will—return your thoughts to God's love. Then, take your concerns to Him in prayer, and to the best of your ability, leave them there. Whatever "it" is, God is big enough to handle it. Let Him. Now.

When something robs you of your peace of mind, ask yourself if it is worth the energy you are expending on it. If not, then put it out of your mind in an act of discipline. Every time the thought of "it" returns, refuse it.

Kay Arthur

Pet Facts: So Many Dogs

There are more than 350 different breeds of dogs. Can you name them all? If so, you're one of the greatest dog experts in the world!

NEVER GIVE UP

Even though good people may be bothered by trouble seven times, they are never defeated.

Proverbs 24:16 NCV

D o you sincerely want to live a life that is pleasing to God? If so, you must remember that life is not a sprint, it's a marathon that calls for preparation, determination, and lots of perseverance.

Are you one of those people who doesn't give up easily, or are you quick to bail out when the going gets tough? If you've developed the unfortunate habit of giving up at the first sign of trouble, it's probably time for you to have a heart-to-heart talk with the person you see every time you look in the mirror.

If you're facing a difficult situation, remember this: whatever your problem, God can handle it. Your job is to keep persevering until He does.

Determination and faithfulness are the nails used to build the house of God's dreams.

Barbara Johnson

Pet Facts: Big Parrots Can Live a Long Time

Larger parrots such as the macaws and cockatoos live more than 75 years.

CONTENTMENT NOW

Your life should be free from the love of money. Be satisfied with what you have, for He Himself has said, I will never leave you or forsake you.

Hebrews 13:5 HCSB

Where can we find contentment? Is it a result of being wealthy or famous? Nope. Genuine contentment is a gift from God to those who trust Him and follow His commandments.

If we don't find contentment in God, we will never find it anywhere else. But, if we seek Him and obey Him, we will be blessed with joyful, peaceful, meaningful lives. When God dwells at the center of our lives, peace and contentment will belong to us just as surely as we belong to God.

We might occasionally be able to change our circumstances, but only God can change our hearts.

Beth Moore

God's Amazing Animals: Don't Stand Behind a Giraffe!

An adult giraffe's kick is so powerful that it can defend itself against any animal, even a lion!

GUARDING OUR HEARTS AND MINDS

Finally brothers, whatever is true, whatever is honorable, whatever is just, whatever is pure, whatever is lovely, whatever is commendable— if there is any moral excellence and if there is any praise—dwell on these things.

Philippians 4:8 HCSB

You are near and dear to God. He loves you more than you can imagine, and He wants the very best for you. And one more thing: God wants you to guard your heart.

Every day, you are faced with choices . . . lots of them. You can do the right thing, or not. You can tell the truth, or not. You can be kind, and generous, and obedient. Or not.

Your mind and your heart will usually tell you the right thing to do. And if you listen to your parents and grandparents, they will help you, too, by teaching you God's rules. Then, you will learn that doing the right thing is always better than doing the wrong thing. And, by obeying God's rules, you will guard your heart by giving it to His Son Jesus.

God's Amazing Animals: A Very Long Mole Hole!

A mole can dig a tunnel 300 feet long in a single night.

UNIQUELY YOU

For you made us only a little lower than God, and you crowned us with glory and honor.

Psalm 8:5 NLT

How many people in the world are exactly like you? The only person in the world who's exactly like you . . . is you! And that means you're special: special to God, special to your family, special to your friends, and a special addition to God's wonderful world!

But sometimes, when you are tired, angry, dejected, or depressed, you may not feel very special. In fact, you may decide that you're the ugliest duckling in the pond, a not-very-special person . . . but whenever you think like that, you're mistaken.

The Bible says that God made you in "an amazing and wonderful way." So the next time that you start feeling like you don't measure up, remember this: when God made all the people of the earth, He only made one you. You're incredibly valuable to God, and that means that you should think of yourself as a V.I.P. (Very Important Person). God wants you to have the best, and you deserve the best . . . you're worth it!

God's Amazing Animals: Need Some Water?

An elephant can smell water up to 3 miles away.

WHAT GOD REQUIRES

But he's already made it plain how to live, what to do, what God is looking for in men and women. It's quite simple: Do what is fair and just to your neighbor, be compassionate and loyal in your love, and don't take yourself too seriously—take God seriously.

Micah 6:8 MSG

When Jesus was tempted by Satan, the Master's response was clear. Jesus chose to worship the Lord and serve Him only. We, as followers of Christ, must follow in His footsteps.

When we place God in a position of secondary importance, we do ourselves great harm, and we put ourselves at great risk. But when we place God squarely in the center of our lives, when we walk humbly and obediently with Him, we are blessed and we are protected.

God's Amazing Animals: How Long Do Rabbits Live?

Under the right conditions, rabbits can live to be about 10 years old.

THE LOVE OF MONEY . . .

For the love of money is a root of all sorts of evil, and some by longing for it have wandered away from the faith and pierced themselves with many griefs. But flee from these things, you man of God, and pursue righteousness, godliness, faith, love, perseverance and gentleness.

1 Timothy 6:11 NASB

Our society is in love with money and the things that money can buy. God is not. God cares about people, not possessions, and so must we. We must, to the best of our abilities, love our neighbors as ourselves, and we must, to the best of our abilities, resist the mighty temptation to place possessions ahead of people.

Money, in and of itself, is not evil; worshipping money is. So today, as you play the game of life and prioritize matters of importance, remember that God is almighty, but the dollar is not. If we worship God, we are blessed. But if we worship "the almighty dollar," we are inevitably punished because of our misplaced priorities—and our punishment inevitably comes sooner rather than later.

Pet Facts: So Many Dogs!

There are almost 65 million dogs in the United States.

GOD HAS PLANS FOR YOU

If we live by the Spirit, we must also follow the Spirit.
Galatians 5:25 HCSB

God has plans for your life, wonderful, surprising plans . . . but He won't force those plans upon you. To the contrary, He has given you free will, the ability to make decisions on your own. Now, it's up to you to make those decisions wisely.

If you seek to live in accordance with God's plan for your life, you will study His Word, you will be attentive to His instructions, and you will be watchful for His signs. You will associate with fellow believers who, by their words and actions, will encourage your spiritual growth. You will assiduously avoid those two terrible temptations: the temptation to sin and the temptation to squander time. And finally, you will listen carefully, even reverently, to the conscience that God has placed in your heart.

God intends to use you in wonderful, unexpected ways if you let Him. Let Him.

God's Amazing Animals:
Our Oceans Have Many Different Kinds of Whales

Whales come in many different types. In fact, there are about 80 different kinds of whales.

GODLY THOUGHTS, GODLY ACTIONS

Commit your activities to the Lord and your plans will be achieved.

Proverbs 16:3 HCSB

Our thoughts have the power to lift us up or drag us down; they have the power to energize us or deplete us, to inspire us to greater accomplishments, or to make those accomplishments impossible.

God intends that you experience joy and abundance, but He will not impose His joy upon you; you must accept it for yourself. It's up to you to celebrate the life that God has given you by focusing your mind upon "whatever is of good repute" (Philippians 4:8). So today, spend more time thinking about God's blessings, and less time fretting about the minor inconveniences of life. Then, take time to thank the Giver of all things good for gifts that are glorious, miraculous, and eternal.

It is the thoughts and intents of the heart that shape a person's life.

John Eldredge

God's Amazing Animals: When Tigers Go Hunting

Tigers usually hunt alone at nighttime.

THE POWER OF WILLING HANDS

A lazy person will end up poor, but a hard worker will become rich.

Proverbs 10:4 NCV

God's Word teaches us the value of hard work. In his second letter to the Thessalonians, Paul warns, "…if anyone will not work, neither shall he eat" (3:10 NKJV). And the Book of Proverbs proclaims, "A person who doesn't work hard is just like someone who destroys things" (18:9 NCV). In short, God has created a world in which diligence is rewarded but sloth is not. So, whatever it is that you choose to do, do it with enthusiasm and dedication.

Hard work is not simply a proven way to get ahead; it's also part of God's game plan for you. God did not create you for a life of mediocrity; He created you for far greater things. Reaching for greater things usually requires work, which is perfectly fine with God. After all, He knows that you're up to the task, and He has big plans for you if you possess a loving heart and willing hands.

Pet Facts: Cat Sounds

Cats can make over a hundred vocal sounds, while dogs have only about ten.

FAITHFULNESS AND FOCUS

But if from there you seek the LORD your God, you will find him if you look for him with all your heart and with all your soul.

Deuteronomy 4:29 NIV

God deserves your best. Is He getting it? Do you make an appointment with your Heavenly Father each day? Do you carve out moments when He receives your undivided attention? Or is your devotion to Him fleeting, distracted, and sporadic?

When you acquire the habit of focusing your heart and mind squarely upon God's intentions for your life, He will guide your steps and bless your endeavors. But if you allow distractions to take priority over your relationship with God, they will—and you will pay a price for your mistaken priorities.

Today, focus upon God's Word and upon His will for your life. When you do, you'll be amazed at how quickly everything else comes into focus, too.

Pet Facts: Why Max?

Some dog experts say that Max is the most popular name for dogs. Do you know a dog named Max? If so, why was Max named Max?

UNDERSTANDING CHRIST'S LOVE

And I pray that you and all God's holy people will have the power to understand the greatness of Christ's love—how wide and how long and how high and how deep that love is. Christ's love is greater than anyone can ever know, but I pray that you will be able to know that love. Then you can be filled with the fullness of God.

Ephesians 3:18–19 NCV

Christ's love for you is personal. He loves you so much that He gave His life in order that you might spend all eternity with Him. Christ loves you individually and intimately; His is a love unbounded by time or circumstance.

Are you willing to experience an intimate relationship with Him? Your Savior is waiting patiently; don't make Him wait a single minute longer. Embrace His love today. After all, you can never be sure what tomorrow may bring, but today is yours. Accept Christ's love today.

God's Amazing Animals: How Can They Do It?

Amazingly, a woodpecker can peck 20 times in a second.

THE TIME IS NOW

Hard work means prosperity; only fools idle away their time.

Proverbs 12:11 NLT

Are you one of those girls who puts things off until the last minute? Do you waste time doing things that don't matter very much while putting off the important things until it's too late to do the job right? If so, it's now time to start making better choices.

It may seem like you've got all the time in the world to do the things you need to do, but time is shorter than you think. Time here on earth is limited . . . use it or lose it!

Our time is short! The time we can invest for God, in creative things, in receiving our fellowmen for Christ, is short!

Billy Graham

God's Amazing Animals: A Fun Frog Fact

Instead of drinking water, frogs soak it into their body through their skin.

FAITH ON FIRE

I tell you the truth, whoever believes in me will do the same things that I do. Those who believe will do even greater things than these, because I am going to the Father.

John 14:12 NCV

John Wesley advised, "Catch on fire with enthusiasm and people will come for miles to watch you burn." His words still ring true. When we fan the flames of enthusiasm for Christ, our faith serves as a beacon to others.

Our world desperately needs faithful believers who share the Good News of Jesus with joyful exuberance. Be such a believer. The world desperately needs your enthusiasm, and just as importantly, you need the experience of sharing it.

God's Amazing Animals: A Gorilla Can Catch a Cold . . . from You!

Gorillas can catch colds (and other illnesses) from people. So if you plan on shaking hands with a gorilla (which we certainly don't advise), use hand sanitizer first!

BEYOND BLAME

When they continued to ask Jesus their question, he raised up and said, "Anyone here who has never sinned can throw the first stone at her."

John 8:7 NCV

To blame others for our own problems isn't smart. Yet blaming others is so easy to do and improving ourselves is so much harder. So instead of solving problems ourselves, we are tempted to do otherwise; we are tempted to fret over the perceived unfairness of life while doing precious little else.

Are you looking for an ironclad formula for problem-solving that will leave you happier, healthier, wealthier, and wiser? Here it is: don't play the blame game—because to play it is to lose it.

A person may make mistakes, but he isn't a failure until he starts blaming someone else.

John Wooden

God's Amazing Animals: Cheetah Fast

The cheetah is the fastest land mammal in the world. It lives in Africa and weighs about 120 pounds when it's fully grown. At top speed, it can run at 70 miles per hour!

ALWAYS PLAY FAIRLY

The Lord hates dishonest scales, but he is pleased with honest weights.

Proverbs 11:1 NCV

It has been said on many occasions and in many ways that honesty is the best policy. For believers, it is far more important to note that honesty is God's policy. And if we are to be servants worthy of our Savior, Jesus Christ, we must be honest and forthright in our communications with others.

Sometimes, honesty is difficult; sometimes, honesty is painful; always, honesty is God's commandment. In the Book of Exodus, God did not command, "Thou shalt not bear false witness when it is convenient." And He didn't say, "Thou shalt not bear false witness most of the time." God said, "Thou shalt not bear false witness against thy neighbor." Period.

Sometime soon, perhaps even today, you will be tempted to bend the truth or perhaps even to break it. Resist that temptation. Truth is God's way . . . and it must also be yours. Period.

Pet Facts: The Most Popular Bird Pets

Parakeets, canaries, and finches are the most popular kinds of bird pets.

GOT QUESTIONS?

An indecisive man is unstable in all his ways.

James 1:8 HCSB

God doesn't explain Himself to us with the clarity that we humans would prefer (think about this: if God did explain Himself with perfect clarity, we wouldn't have enough brainpower to understand the explanation that He gave!).

When innocent people are hurt, we question God because we can't figure out exactly what He's doing, or why. Since we can't fully answer that question now, we must trust in God's love, God's wisdom, and God's plan.

And while we're waiting for that wonderful day when all our questions will be answered (in heaven), we should use the time that we have here on earth to help the people who need it most.

I am truly grateful that faith enables me to move past the question of "Why?"

Zig Ziglar

Pet Facts: Boney Cats

A cat's body has more than 230 bones (a human has about 206).

ENOUGH IS ENOUGH

Let your character be free from the love of money, being content with what you have; for He Himself has said, "I will never desert you, nor will I ever forsake you."

Hebrews 13:5 NASB

Ours is a world that glorifies material possessions. Christians, of course, should not. As believers who have been touched and transformed by the grace of a risen Savior, we must never allow the things of this earth to distance us from our sense of God's presence and the direction of God's hand. If we are to enjoy the peace and abundance that God has promised us, we must reign in our desire for more and more; we must acknowledge that when it comes to earthly possessions, enough is always enough.

The key to contentment is to consider. Consider who you are and be satisfied with that. Consider what you have and be satisfied with that. Consider what God's doing and be satisfied with that.

Luci Swindoll

God's Amazing Animals:
What Kind of Animal Is a Frog?

Frog are amphibians. That means they live on land or in water.

BE THANKFUL NOW!

And whatever you do, in word or in deed, do everything in the name of the Lord Jesus, giving thanks to God the Father through Him.

Colossians 3:17 HCSB

Are you a girl with a seriously thankful attitude? Hopefully so! After all, you've got plenty of things to be thankful for. Even during those times when you're angry, bored, frustrated, or tired, you're a very lucky person.

Who has given you all the blessings you enjoy? Your parents are responsible, of course, and so are your teachers, coaches, and friends. But all of your blessings really start with God. That's why you should say "Thank You" to God many times each day. He's given you so much . . . so thank Him, starting now.

It is always possible to be thankful for what is given rather than to complain about what is not given. One or the other becomes a habit of life.

Elisabeth Elliot

God's Amazing Animals: How Dolphins Talk

Dolphins communicate by clicking, whistling, and other sounds.

LIVING IN AN ANXIOUS WORLD

Don't fret or worry. Instead of worrying, pray. Let petitions and praises shape your worries into prayers, letting God know your concerns. Before you know it, a sense of God's wholeness, everything coming together for good, will come and settle you down. It's wonderful what happens when Christ displaces worry at the center of your life.

Philippians 4:6-7 MSG

We live in a world that often breeds anxiety and fear. When we come face-to-face with tough times, we may fall prey to discouragement, doubt, or depression. But our Father in heaven has other plans. God has promised that we may lead lives of abundance, not anxiety. In fact, His Word instructs us to "be anxious for nothing." But how can we put our fears to rest? By taking those fears to God and leaving them there.

As you face the challenges of everyday living, do you find yourself becoming anxious, troubled, discouraged, or fearful? If so, turn every one of your concerns over to your Heavenly Father. The same God who created the universe will comfort you if you ask Him . . . so ask Him and trust Him. Now.

God's Amazing Animals: An Unusual Way to Use a Tongue!

A giraffe can clean its ears with its 21-inch tongue!

LOVING GOD, LOVING PEOPLE

Jesus replied, "'Love the Lord your God with all your heart and with all your soul and with all your mind.' This is the first and greatest commandment. And the second is like it: 'Love your neighbor as yourself.' All the Law and the Prophets hang on these two commandments."

Matthew 22:37-40 NIV

Christ's words are clear: He instructs us to love the Lord with all our hearts and to love our neighbors as we love ourselves. But sometimes, despite our best intentions, we fall short. When we become embittered with ourselves, with our neighbors, or most especially with God, we disobey the One who gave His life for us. And we bring inevitable, needless suffering into our lives.

In 1 Corinthians 13, we are told that love is the foundation upon which all our relationships are to be built—our relationships with others and our relationship with our Creator. May we fill our hearts with love; may we never yield to bitterness. And may we praise the Son of God who, in His infinite wisdom, made love His greatest commandment.

God's Amazing Animals: Ants Have No Time for Naps!

Ants are so busy that they don't take naps. In fact, they don't sleep at all!

BIG REWARDS WHEN YOU DO THE RIGHT THING

Do you want to be counted wise, to build a reputation for wisdom? Here's what you do: Live well, live wisely, live humbly. It's the way you live, not the way you talk, that counts.

James 3:13 MSG

If you open up a dictionary, you'll see that the word "wisdom" means "using good judgment, and knowing what is true," But there's more to it than that. It's not enough to know what's right—if you want to be wise, you must also do what's right.

The Bible promises that when you do smart things, you'll earn big rewards (and it also promises, by the way, that if you do dumb things, you definitely won't get big rewards).

So slow down and think about things before you do them, not after. It's the smart way to live.

Let us not be content to wait and see what will happen, but give us the determination to make the right things happen.

Peter Marshall

God's Amazing Animals: Tigers Can Jump!

Tigers can easily jump over 15 feet in length. And, they can jump much farther than that if they need to.

THAT LITTLE VOICE

For God is pleased with you when, for the sake of your conscience, you patiently endure unfair treatment.

1 Peter 2:19 NLT

When you know that you're doing what's right, you'll feel better about yourself. Why? Because you have a little voice in your head called your conscience. Your conscience is the feeling that tells you whether something is right or wrong—and it's a feeling that makes you feel better about yourself when you know you've done the right thing.

Your conscience is an important tool. Pay attention to it! The more you listen to your conscience, the easier it is to behave yourself.

So here's great advice: first, slow down long enough to figure out the right thing to do—and then do it! When you do, you'll be very glad you did.

God's Amazing Animals: A Bison's Fur Coat

A bison's thick fur offers great protection against harsh winters. A bison's fur is so thick that a bison can be covered in snow and still stay warm.

BE HUMBLE

We love because He first loved us.

1 John 4:19 HCSB

As we consider Christ's sacrifice on the cross, we should be profoundly humbled. So today, as you come to Christ in prayer, you should do so in a spirit of humble devotion.

Christ humbled Himself on a cross—for you. He shed His blood—for you. He has offered to walk with you through this life and throughout all eternity. And that's a promise you can depend on today, tomorrow, and forever. As you approach Him today in prayer, think about His sacrifice and His grace. And be humble.

If you know who you are in Christ, your personal ego is not an issue.

Beth Moore

God's Amazing Animals: How Dolphins Breathe

Dolphins breathe through a hole on top of their heads.

WORSHIPPING CHRIST

He is not here, but He has been resurrected!

Luke 24:6 HCSB

God has a wonderful game plan for your life, and an important part of that plan includes worship. We should never deceive ourselves: every life is based upon some form of worship. The question is not whether we worship, but what we worship.

Some of us choose to worship God. The result is a plentiful harvest of joy, peace, and abundance. Others distance themselves from God by foolishly worshipping earthly possessions and personal gratification. To do so is a mistake of profound proportions.

Have you accepted the grace of God's only begotten Son? Then worship Him. Worship Him today and every day. Worship Him with sincerity and thanksgiving. Write His name on your heart and rest assured that He, too, has written your name on His.

God's Amazing Animals: Gorillas Are Smart!

Gorillas are very intelligent animals. They can learn how to use tools, and a few genius gorillas have even learned sign language while living at the zoo!

THE RIGHT THING

For the Kingdom of God is not just fancy talk; it is living by God's power.

1 Corinthians 4:20 NLT

If you're willing to stand up for the things you believe in, you'll feel better about yourself and you'll make better choices. But if you're one person on Sunday morning and a different person throughout the rest of the week, you'll be doing yourself—and your conscience—a big disservice.

The moment that you decide to stand up for your beliefs, you can no longer be a lukewarm, halfhearted Christian. And, when you are no longer a lukewarm Christian, God rejoices (and the devil doesn't).

So stand up for your beliefs. And remember this: in the battle of good versus evil, the devil never takes a day off . . . and neither should you.

God's Amazing Animals:
Elephants Need Plenty of Water

An elephant can use its tusks to dig for ground water. An adult elephant needs to drink at least 50 gallons of water each day.

TRUSTING GOD'S LOVE

Who can separate us from the love of Christ? Can affliction or anguish or persecution or famine or nakedness or danger or sword? . . . No, in all these things we are more than victorious through Him who loved us.

Romans 8:35,37 HCSB

The Bible makes it clear: God's got a very big plan and you're an important part of it. But here's the catch: God won't force His plans upon you; you've got to figure things out for yourself.

As a follower of Christ, you should ask yourself this question: "How closely can I make my plans match God's plans?" The more closely you manage to follow the path that God intends for your life, the better.

Do you have questions or concerns about the future? Take them to God in prayer. Do you have hopes and expectations? Talk to God about your dreams. Are you carefully planning for the days and weeks ahead? Consult God as you establish your priorities. Turn every concern over to God, and sincerely seek His guidance—prayerfully, earnestly, and often. Then, listen for His answers . . . and trust the answers that He gives.

God's Amazing Animals: Ferrets Like to Snooze

Ferrets sleep around 20 hours a day.

MAKE THE CHOICE TO REJOICE!

My purpose is to give life in all its fullness.

John 10:10 HCSB

Are you a girl who has made the choice to rejoice? Hopefully so. After all, if you're a believer, you have plenty of reasons to be joyful. Yet sometimes, amid the inevitable hustle and bustle of life here on earth, you may lose sight of your blessings as you wrestle with the challenges of everyday life.

Christ made it clear to His followers: He intended that His joy would become their joy. And it still holds true today: Christ intends that His believers share His love with His joy in their hearts.

What does life have in store for you? A world full of possibilities (of course it's up to you to seize them) and God's promise of abundance (of course it's up to you to accept it). So, as you embark upon the next phase of your journey, remember to celebrate the life that God has given you. Your Creator has blessed you beyond measure. Honor Him with your prayers, your words, your deeds, and your joy.

God's Amazing Animals: How to Change a Goldfish's Color

If you keep a goldfish in a dark room, it will become pale!

THE GOLDEN RULE

Here is a simple, rule-of-thumb for behavior: Ask yourself what you want people to do for you, then grab the initiative and do it for them. Add up God's Law and Prophets and this is what you get.

Matthew 7:12 MSG

Would you like to make the world a better place? If so, you can start by practicing the Golden Rule.

Jesus said, "Do to others what you want them to do to you" (Matthew 7:12 NCV). That means that you should treat other people in the very same way that you want to be treated. That's the Golden Rule.

Is the Golden Rule your rule, or is it just another Bible verse that goes in one ear and out the other? Jesus made Himself perfectly clear: He instructed you to treat other people in the same way that you want to be treated. But sometimes, especially when you're feeling pressure from friends, or when you're tired or upset, obeying the Golden Rule can seem like an impossible task—but it's not. So if you want to know how to treat other people, ask the person you see every time you look into the mirror.

God's Amazing Animals: Why Tigers Don't Need Flashlights

Tigers can see 6 times better at night than people do.

HE'S LISTENING

One day Jesus told his disciples a story to illustrate their need for constant prayer and to show them that they must never give up.

Luke 18:1 NLT

Are you faced with a difficult choice or an important decision? Then pray about it. If you talk to God sincerely and often, He won't lead you astray. Instead, God will guide you and help you make more intelligent choices . . . if you take the time to talk with Him.

If you have questions about whether you should do something or not, pray about it. If there is something you're worried about, ask God to comfort you. If you're having trouble with your relationships, ask God to help you sort things out. As you pray more, you'll discover that God is always near and that He's always ready to hear from you. So don't worry about things; pray about them. God is waiting . . . and listening!

Pet Facts: Cats Like to Sleep

Cats get plenty of sleep. They conserve energy by sleeping up to 14 hours a day.

EACH DAY IS A GIFT

How happy are those who can live in your house, always singing your praises. How happy are those who are strong in the Lord . . . .

Psalm 84:4-5 NLT

God wants you to have a happy, joyful life. But that doesn't mean that you'll be happy all the time. Sometimes, you won't feel like feeling happy, and when you don't, your attitude won't be very good.

When you're feeling a little tired or sad, here's something to remember: This day is a gift from God. And it's up to you to enjoy this day by trying to be cheerful, helpful, courteous, and well behaved. How can you do these things? A good place to start is by doing your best to think good thoughts.

When we do what is right, we have contentment, peace, and happiness.

Beverly LaHaye

Pet Facts: The First Astronaut Had Four Legs

The first space astronaut was a Russian dog named Laikia.

GIVING GOD YOUR COMPLETE ATTENTION

Worship the Lord your God and . . . serve Him only.
Matthew 4:10 HCSB

Nineteenth-century clergyman Edwin Hubbel Chapin warned, "Neutral people are the devil's allies." His words were true then, and they're true now. Neutrality in the face of evil is a sin. Yet all too often, we fail to fight evil, not because we are neutral, but because we are shortsighted: we don't fight the devil because we don't recognize his handiwork.

If we are to recognize evil and fight it, we must pay careful attention. We must pay attention to God's Word, and we must pay attention to the realities of everyday life. When we look at life with eyes and hearts that are attuned to God's Word, we can no longer be neutral Christians. And when we are no longer neutral, God rejoices while the devil despairs.

The greatest enemy of holiness is not passion; it is apathy.

John Eldredge

God's Amazing Animals: How Giraffes Digest Food

Giraffes have four stomachs. The extra stomachs help them digest food.

FINDING PURPOSE THROUGH CHARITY

Happy is the person who thinks about the poor. When trouble comes, the Lord will save him.

Psalm 41:1 NCV

God's Word commands us to be generous, compassionate servants to those who need our help. As believers, we have been richly blessed by our Creator. We, in turn, are called to share our gifts, our possessions, and our talents.

Corrie ten Boom correctly observed, "The measure of a life is not its duration but its donation." These words remind us that the quality of our lives is determined not by what we are able to take from others, but instead by what we are able to share with others.

The thread of generosity is woven into the very fabric of Christ's teachings. If we are to be His disciples, then we, too, must be cheerful, generous, courageous givers. Our Savior expects no less from us. And He deserves no less.

Pet Facts: Plenty of People Own Pet Birds

It is estimated that over 40 million Americans own pet birds.

REAL FAITH

For in it God's righteousness is revealed from faith to faith, just as it is written: The righteous will live by faith.

Romans 1:17 HCSB

In the game of life, there are winners and losers. The winners are the folks who choose to form a genuine, life-altering relationship with Jesus Christ. Jesus wants to have a real relationship with you. Are you willing to have a real relationship with Him? Unless you can answer this question with a resounding "Yes," you may miss out on some wonderful things.

This day offers yet another opportunity to behave yourself like a real Christian. And it's yet another chance to put God first in your life. When you do, God will guide your steps and bless your endeavors . . . forever.

God's Amazing Animals:
Where Polar Bears Live, and Why They Live There

Polar bears live in the Arctic. It's cold there, which is exactly how the polar bears like it.

FRIENDS YOU CAN TRUST

Friends come and friends go, but a true friend sticks by you like family.

Proverbs 18:24 MSG

All lasting friendships are built upon both honesty and trust. Without trust, friends soon drift apart. But with trust, friends can stay friends for a lifetime.

As Christians, we should always try to be trustworthy friends. And, we should be thankful for the people who are loyal friends to us. When we treat other people with honesty and respect, we not only make more friends, but we also keep the friendships we've already made.

Do you want friends you can trust? Then start by being a friend they can trust. That's the way to make your friendships strong, stronger, and strongest!

Don't bypass the potential for meaningful friendships just because of differences. Explore them. Embrace them. Love them.

Luci Swindoll

God's Amazing Animals: A Big Heart with a Slow Beast

A typical whale has a very slow heartbeat compared to other animals. In fact, a whale's heart usually beats less than ten times a minute.

REAL WINNERS DON'T PLAY THE BLAME GAME

People's own foolishness ruins their lives, but in their minds they blame the Lord.

Proverbs 19:3 NCV

When something goes wrong, do you look for somebody to blame? And do you try to blame other people even if you're the one who made the mistake? Hopefully not!

It's silly to try to blame other people for your own mistakes, so don't do it.

If you've done something you're ashamed of, don't look for somebody to blame; look for a way to say, "I'm sorry, and I won't make that same mistake again." Then, do your best to repair the mistake . . . and move on.

You'll never win the blame game, so why even bother to play?

Marie T. Freeman

God's Amazing Animals: About Kangaroos

Kangaroos are found in Australia as well as in New Guinea. There are four different kinds of kangaroos: the red kangaroo, the eastern gray kangaroo, the western gray kangaroo, and the antilopine kangaroo.

GOD WROTE A BOOK

For I am not ashamed of the gospel, because it is God's power for salvation to everyone who believes.

Romans 1:16 HCSB

If you want to know God, you should read the book He wrote. It's called the Bible (of course!), and God uses it to teach you and guide you. The Bible is not like any other book. It is an amazing gift from your Heavenly Father. And it's a gift you need desperately.

D. L. Moody observed, "The Bible was not given to increase our knowledge but to change our lives." God's Holy Word is, indeed, a life-changing, one-of-a-kind treasure. Handle it with care, but more importantly, handle it every day!

If we neglect the Bible, we cannot expect to benefit from the wisdom and direction that result from knowing God's Word.

Vonette Bright

Pet Facts: Is It Parrot-talk or People-talk?

Some parrots are particularly good at imitating human voices. If you own a parrot, can you tell the difference?

WINNERS GET THEIR WISDOM
FROM ABOVE

The Lord says, "I will make you wise and show you where to go. I will guide you and watch over you."

Psalm 32:8 NCV

Your head is undoubtedly filled with a growing collection of valuable information. But, there is much yet to learn. Wisdom is like a savings account: If you add to it consistently, then eventually you'll have a great sum. The secret to success is consistency.

Would you like to be a wise young woman? Then keep learning. Seek wisdom every day, and seek it in the right place. That place, of course, is, first and foremost, the Word of God. And remember this: it's not enough to simply read God's Word; you've also got to live by it.

God's Amazing Animals:
Sheep Can Look Around Without
Turning Their Heads

Sheep can see lots of things beside them, and even some things behind them. So, they can see behind themselves without having to turn their heads.

DAY 162

CONTAGIOUS CHRISTIANITY

All those who stand before others and say they believe in me, I will say before my Father in heaven that they belong to me.

Matthew 10:32 NCV

Genuine, heartfelt Christianity is contagious. If you enjoy a life-altering relationship with God, that relationship will have an impact on others—perhaps a very big impact.

Are you genuinely excited about your faith? And do you make your enthusiasm known to those around you? Or are you a "silent ambassador" for Christ? God's preference is clear: He intends that you stand before others and talk about your faith. So today, make sure to share your faith and your excitement. The world needs both.

The Christian lifestyle is not one of legalistic do's and don'ts, but one that is positive, attractive, and joyful.

Vonette Bright

God's Amazing Animals: Don't Try to Outrun a Bear!

Bears are faster than you think. In fact, a full-grown bear can run as fast as a horse.

ABANDONING THE STATUS QUO

I have come as a light into the world, so that everyone who believes in Me would not remain in darkness.

John 12:46 HCSB

Okay, answer this question honestly: Do you behave differently because of your relationship with Jesus? Or do you behave in pretty much the same way that you would if you weren't a believer? Hopefully, the fact that you've invited Christ to reign over your heart means that you've made BIG changes in your thoughts and your actions.

Doing the right thing is not always easy, especially when you're tired or frustrated. But, doing the wrong thing almost always leads to trouble. And sometimes, it leads to big trouble.

If you're determined to follow "the crowd," you may soon find yourself headed in the wrong direction. So here's some advice: Don't follow the crowd—follow Jesus. And keep following Him every day of your life.

Pet Facts: What Does a Cat Mean When It Purrs?

Usually, purring means that a cat is happy. But cats have also been known to purr loudly when they are upset or in pain.

BARNABAS, THE ENCOURAGING FRIEND

Now Joseph, a Levite of Cyprian birth, who was also called Barnabas by the apostles (which translated means Son of Encouragement)...

Acts 4:36 NASB

Barnabas, a man whose name meant "Son of Encouragement," was a leader in the early Christian church. He was known for his kindness and for his ability to encourage others. Because of Barnabas, many people were introduced to Christ. And today, as believers living in a difficult world, we must seek to imitate the "Son of Encouragement."

We imitate Barnabas when we speak kind words to our families and to our friends. We imitate Barnabas when our actions give credence to our beliefs. We imitate Barnabas when we are generous with our possessions and with our praise. We imitate Barnabas when we give hope to the hopeless and encouragement to the downtrodden.

Today, be like Barnabas: become a source of encouragement to those who cross your path. When you do so, you will quite literally change the world, one person—and one moment—at a time.

Pet Facts: Lots of Fish Lovers

Over 12 million American families own pet fish.

BE CAREFUL!

Be careful! Watch out for attacks from the Devil, your great enemy. He prowls around like a roaring lion, looking for some victim to devour. Take a firm stand against him, and be strong in your faith.

1 Peter 5:8-9 NLT

If you stop to think about it, the cold, hard evidence is right in front of your eyes: you live in a temptation-filled world. The devil is out on the street, hard at work, causing pain and heartache in more ways than ever before. Yep, you live in a temptation nation, a place where the bad guys are working 24/7 to lead you astray. That's why you must remain vigilant. Not only must you resist Satan when he confronts you, but you must also avoid those places where Satan can most easily tempt you.

In 1 Peter 5:8, Peter compares the devil to a hungry lion. What was true in New Testament times is equally true in our own. Satan tempts his prey and then devours them (and it's up to you—and only you—to make sure that you're not one of the ones being devoured!). Satan is determined to win; we must be equally determined that he does not.

God's Amazing Animals: Big Bird, Little Brain

An ostrich's brain is smaller than its eye.

CHOOSING WISELY

I am offering you life or death, blessings or curses. Now, choose life! . . . To choose life is to love the Lord your God, obey him, and stay close to him.

Deuteronomy 30:19-20 NCV

Choices, choices, choices! You've got so many choices to make, and sometimes, making those choices isn't easy. At times you're torn between what you want to do and what you ought to do. When that happens, it's up to you to choose wisely . . . or else!

When you make wise choices, you are rewarded; when you make unwise choices, you must accept the consequences. It's as simple as that. So make sure that your choices are pleasing to God . . . or else!

No matter how many books you read, no matter how many schools you attend, you're never really wise until you start making wise choices.

Marie T. Freeman

God's Amazing Animals: Elephants Are Vegetarians!

Elephants eat plants, lots of plants! In fact, a typical elephant may spend up to 16 hours a day eating leaves, twigs, bamboo, and roots.

SAFETY MATTERS

The prudent see danger and take refuge, but the simple keep going and suffer from it.

Proverbs 27:12 NIV

Nobody can deny the fact that far too many young people behave recklessly at times. Don't you dare be one of them. If your peers try to convince you to do something that is foolish, dangerous, or both, run—don't walk—in the opposite direction.

Maturity and safety go hand in hand. Why? Because a big part of being a mature human being is learning how to look around and think things through before you do something that you might regret later.

As the old saying goes, "Look before you leap." And those words apply whether you're "leaping" by yourself or with a whole bunch of friends. In fact, if you want to live happily ever after, you should look very carefully before you decide whether or not to leap. After all, it's easy to leap, but once you're in the middle of your jump, it's too late to leap back!

God's Amazing Animals:
More Ants Than People? Absolutely!

Some experts have estimated that for every human being in the world there are at least one million ants, and maybe more.

GUIDED BY HONESTY

Good people will be guided by honesty; dishonesty will destroy those who are not trustworthy.

Proverbs 11:3 NCV

Charles Swindoll observed, "Nothing speaks louder or more powerfully than a life of integrity." And, of course, he was right!

Integrity is built slowly over a lifetime. It is a precious thing—difficult to build but easy to tear down. As believers in Christ, we must seek to live each day with discipline, honesty, and faith. When we do, at least two things happen: integrity becomes a habit, and God blesses us because of our obedience to Him.

Living a life of integrity isn't always the easiest way, but it is always the right way. And God clearly intends that it should be our way, too.

God's Amazing Animals:
A Horse Eats Like ... a Horse!

A typical horse that weighs 1,200 pounds will eat about 7 times its own weight every year. That's over 4 tons of food. Hey, that's a lot of hay!

SINCE TOMORROW IS NOT PROMISED

We must do the works of Him who sent Me while it is day. Night is coming when no one can work.

John 9:4 HCSB

The words of John 9:4 remind us that "night is coming" for all of us. But until then, God gives us each day and fills it to the brim with possibilities. The day is presented to us fresh and clean at midnight, free of charge, but we must beware: Today is a non-renewable resource—once it's gone, it's gone forever. Our responsibility, of course, is to use this day in the service of God's will and in accordance with His commandments.

Today, treasure the time that God has given you. And search for the hidden possibilities that God has placed along your path. This day is a priceless gift from your Creator, so use it joyfully and productively. And encourage others to do likewise. After all, night is coming when no one can work . . .

God's Amazing Animals:
Giraffe Babies Have a Hard Landing!

A female giraffe gives birth while standing up. The calf drops approximately 6 feet to the ground, but it is not hurt from the fall.

THE RICH HARVEST

Now this I say, he who sows sparingly will also reap sparingly, and he who sows bountifully will also reap bountifully.

2 Corinthians 9:6 NASB

How can we serve God? By sharing His message and His love with those who cross our paths.

Everywhere we look, or so it seems, the needs are great. And at every turn, it seems, so are the temptations. Still, our challenge is clear: we must love God, obey His commandments, trust His Son, and serve His children. When we place the Lord in His rightful place—at the center of our lives—we will reap a bountiful spiritual harvest that will endure forever.

That's what I love about serving God. In His eyes, there are no little people . . . because there are no big people. We are all on the same playing field.

Joni Eareckson Tada

Pet Facts: Cats Run Fast!

Most cats are fast. A normal adult cat can run about twelve miles per hour, and can sprint for a short while at nearly thirty miles per hour.

JESUS GIVES LIFE

For whoever finds me finds life and receives favor from the LORD.

Proverbs 8:35 NIV

Who's the best friend this world has ever had? Jesus, of course! When you invite Him into your heart, Jesus will be your friend, too . . . your friend forever.

Jesus has offered to share the gifts of everlasting life and everlasting love with the world . . . and with you. If you make mistakes, He'll still be your friend. If you behave badly, He'll still love you. If you feel sorry or sad, He can help you feel better.

Jesus wants you to have a happy, healthy life. He wants you to be generous and kind. He wants you to follow His example. And the rest is up to you. You can do it! And with a friend like Jesus, you will.

God's Amazing Animals:
So Many Birds, So Many Songs!

Some songbirds sing more than 2,000 times each day. Do you think they ever get tired of hearing the same old tunes day after day?

YOUR ROADMAP

Teach me, O Lord, the way of Your statutes, and I shall keep it to the end.

Psalm 119:33 NKJV

As you look to the future and decide upon the direction of your life, what will you use as your roadmap? Will you trust God's Holy Word and use it as an indispensable tool to guide your steps? Or will you choose a different map to guide your steps? The map you choose will determine the quality of your journey and its ultimate destination.

The Bible is the ultimate guide for life; make it your guidebook as well. When you do, you can be comforted in the knowledge that your steps are guided by a Source of wisdom and truth that never fails.

The Bible was not given to increase our knowledge but to change our lives.

D. L. Moody

Pet Facts: Some Favorite Dog Breeds

Here are some favorite dog breeds: Bulldog, Collie, Golden Retriever, German Shepherd, Greyhound, Chihuahua, Labrador Retriever, Boxer, and Cocker Spaniel.

USING TIME WISELY

Teach us to number our days carefully so that we may develop wisdom in our hearts.

Psalm 90:12 HCSB

An important element of our service to God is the way that we choose to spend the time He has entrusted to us. Each waking moment holds the potential to do a good deed, to say a kind word, or to offer a heartfelt prayer. Our challenge, as believers, is to use our time wisely in the service of God's work and in accordance with His plan for our lives.

Each day is a special treasure to be savored and celebrated. May we—as Christians who have so much to celebrate—never fail to praise our Creator by rejoicing in this glorious day, and by using it wisely.

God's Amazing Animals: A Very Talented Bird

Ostriches are the world's biggest birds. They can kick like a mule, give a realistic imitation of a lion's roar, and hiss like a snake. That's talent!

A GOD OF POSSIBILITIES

But Jesus looked at them and said, "With men this is impossible, but with God all things are possible."

Matthew 19:26 HCSB

If you really want to know God, you must be willing to worship Him seven days a week, not just on Sunday.

God has a wonderful plan for your life, and an important part of that plan includes the time that you set aside for praise and worship. Every life, including yours, is based upon some form of worship. The question is not whether you will worship, but what you worship.

If you choose to worship God, you will receive a king-sized harvest of blessings. But if you distance yourself from God, you're making a huge mistake. So do this: Worship God today and every day. Worship Him with sincerity and thanksgiving. Write His name on your heart and rest assured that He, too, has written your name on His.

God's Amazing Animals:
Turtles Depend on Their Shells

Turtles have a hard shell that protects them against enemies. This upper shell is called a "carapace." Turtles also have a lower shell called a "plastron."

LIES CAN LEAD TO TROUBLE

Your heart must not be troubled. Believe in God; believe also in Me.

John 14:1 HCSB

When we break the rules by telling a lie, trouble starts. Lots of trouble. But when we tell the truth—and nothing but the truth—we stop Old Man Trouble in his tracks.

When we always tell the truth, we make our worries smaller, not bigger. And that's precisely what God wants us to do.

So, if you'd like to have fewer worries and more happiness, tell the truth, the whole truth, nothing but the truth, all the time. When you do, you'll make many of your worries disappear altogether. And that's the truth!

Integrity of heart is indispensable.

John Calvin

God's Amazing Animals: More Sheep Than People

Australia has a population of 17 million people and 150 million sheep.

PRAYERFUL HEARTS AND WILLING HANDS

So you may walk in the way of goodness, and keep to the paths of righteousness. For the upright will dwell in the land, and the blameless will remain in it.

Proverbs 2:20-21 NKJV

The old adage is both familiar and true: We must pray as if everything depended upon God, but work as if everything depended upon us. Yet sometimes, when we are tired or discouraged, we may allow our worries to sap our energy and our hope. God has other intentions. God intends that we pray for things, and He intends that we be willing to work for the things that we pray for. More importantly, God intends that our work should become His work.

If you have concerns about the inevitable challenges of everyday living, take those concerns to God in prayer. He will guide your steps, He will calm your fears, and He will reward your efforts.

Pet Facts: What Dogs Hear

Dogs have great hearing! They can swivel their ears like radar dishes, and they can find the source of a sound in less than a tenth of a second!

QUIET CHARITY

Be careful not to practice your righteousness in front of people, to be seen by them. Otherwise, you will have no reward from your Father in heaven.

Matthew 6:1 HCSB

Hymn writer Fanny Crosby wrote, "To God be the glory; great thing He hath done!" But sometimes, because we are imperfect human beings, we seek the glory. Sometimes, when we do good deeds, we seek to glorify our achievements in a vain attempt to build ourselves up in the eyes of our neighbors. To do so is a profound mistake.

God's Word gives specific instructions about how we should approach our acts of charity: The glory must go to God, not to us. All praise belongs to the Giver of all good gifts: our Father in heaven. We are simply conduits for His generosity, and we must remain humble . . . extremely humble.

We can't do everything, but can we do anything more valuable than invest ourselves in another?

Elisabeth Elliot

Pet Facts: Cats Are Clean!

Cats like to clean themselves, so they spend lots of time licking their coats to keep them clean.

TODAY'S HAPPINESS

But happy are those . . . whose hope is in the LORD their God.

Psalm 146:5 NLT

If we could decide to be happy "once and for all," life would be so much simpler, but it doesn't seem to work that way. If we want happiness to last, we need to create good thoughts every day that we live. Yesterday's good thoughts don't count . . . we've got to think more good thoughts today.

Each new day is a gift from God, so treat it that way. Think about it like this: today is another wonderful chance to celebrate God's gifts.

So celebrate—starting now—and keep celebrating forever!

If our hearts have been attuned to God through an abiding faith in Christ, the result will be joyous optimism and good cheer.

Billy Graham

God's Amazing Animals: A Very Light Bird

A hummingbird never needs to go on a diet because it's already so thin. In fact, a hummingbird weighs less than a small coin!

THE SEARCH FOR WISDOM

But if any of you needs wisdom, you should ask God for it. He is generous and enjoys giving to all people, so he will give you wisdom.

James 1:5 NCV

Are you a girl who seeks the wisdom that only God can give? If so, ask Him for it! If you ask God for guidance, He will not withhold it. If you petition Him sincerely, and if you genuinely seek to form a relationship with Him, your Heavenly Father will guide your steps and enlighten your heart. But be forewarned: You will not acquire God's wisdom without obeying His commandments. Why? Because God's wisdom is more than just a collection of thoughts; it is, first and foremost, a way of life.

Wisdom is as wisdom does. So if you sincerely seek God's wisdom, don't be satisfied to learn something; make up your mind to become something. And then, as you allow God to remake you in the image of His Son, you will most surely become wise.

God's Amazing Animals:
Squirrels Plant Many of the Trees They Climb In

Millions of trees are accidentally planted by squirrels that bury nuts and then forget where they hid them.

GIVING AN ACCOUNT OF OURSELVES

Yes, each of us will have to give a personal account to God.

Romans 14:12 NLT

For most of us, it can be a scary thought: one day, we'll come face-to-face with our Heavenly Father, and we'll be called to account for our actions here on earth. Our personal histories will certainly not be surprising to God; He already knows everything about us. But the full scope of our activities may be surprising to us: some of us will be pleasantly surprised; others will not be.

Today, do whatever you can to ensure that your thoughts and your deeds are pleasing to your Creator. Because you will, at some point in the future, be called to account for your actions. And the future may be sooner than you think.

Don't worry about what you do not understand. Worry about what you do understand in the Bible but do not live by.

Corrie ten Boom

Pet Facts: That's a Very Big Litter

In 2005, Tia, a mastiff, had an amazing litter: 24 cute puppies!

THE PERSON IN THE MIRROR

For you made us only a little lower than God, and you crowned us with glory and honor.

Psalm 8:5 NLT

Do you really like the person you see when you look into the mirror? You should! After all, the person in the mirror is a very special person who is made—and loved—by God.

In fact, you are loved in many, many ways: God loves you, your parents love you, and your family loves you, for starters. So you should love yourself, too.

So here's something to think about: since God thinks you're special, and since so many people think you're special, isn't it about time for you to agree with them? Of course it is! It's time to say, "You're very wonderful and very special," to the person you see in the mirror.

Pet Facts: Wild Dogs Bark Less

Many wild dogs bark less than their domesticated counterparts. But if you ever bump into a wild dog, beware: its bite is probably much worse than its bark.

IF YOU THINK YOU CAN

Though a righteous man falls seven times, he will get up, but the wicked will stumble into ruin.

Proverbs 24:16 HCSB

If you think you can do something, then you can probably do it. If you think you can't do something, then you probably won't do it.

So remember this: if you're having a little trouble getting something done, don't get mad, don't get frustrated, don't get discouraged, and don't give up. Just keep trying . . . and believe in yourself.

When you try hard—and keep trying hard—you can really do amazing things . . . but if you quit at the first sign of trouble, you'll miss out. So here's a good rule to follow: when you have something that you want to finish, finish it . . . and finish it sooner rather than later.

We are all on our way somewhere. We'll get there if we just keep going.

Barbara Johnson

God's Amazing Animals:
Hens Don't Lay Around . . . They're Busy!

An average hen can lay 19 dozen eggs in a year. Breakfast anyone?

EVERY MOMENT MATTERS

Lord, tell me when the end will come and how long I will live. Let me know how long I have. You have given me only a short life . . . . Everyone's life is only a breath.

Psalm 39:4–5 NCV

Every day, like every life, is composed of moments. Each moment of your life holds within it the potential to seek God's will and to serve His purposes. If you are wise, you will try to do both.

An important part of wisdom is the wise use of time. How will you invest your time today? Will you savor the moments of your life, or will you squander them? Will you use your time as an instrument of God's will, or will you allow commonplace distractions to rule your day and your life?

The gift of time is a gift from God. Treat it as if it were a precious, fleeting, one-of-a-kind treasure. Because it is.

Frustration is not the will of God. There is time to do anything and everything that God wants us to do.

Elisabeth Elliot

God's Amazing Animals: Rabbits Are Vegetarians!

What do rabbits like to eat? Rabbits like to eat plants, not meat.

MAKING THE MOST OF OUR TALENTS

Do not neglect the gift that is in you.

1 Timothy 4:14 HCSB

Face it: you've got a collection of talents that need to be improved. All people possess special gifts—bestowed from the Father above—and you are no exception. But, your gift is no guarantee of success; it must be cultivated—by you—or it will go unused . . . and God's gift to you will be squandered.

Today, make a promise to yourself that you will earnestly seek to discover the talents that God has given you. Then, nourish those talents and make them grow. Finally, vow to share your gifts with the world for as long as God gives you the power to do so. After all, the best way to say "Thank You" for God's gifts is to use them.

You are the only person on earth who can use your ability.

Zig Ziglar

Pet Facts: Is Your Cat Right-handed or Left-handed?

A cat can be either right-pawed or left-pawed. Do you know which hand is your cat's best hand?

WORDS WORTHY OF OUR SAVIOR

When you talk, do not say harmful things, but say what people need—words that will help others become stronger. Then what you say will do good to those who listen to you.

Ephesians 4:29 NCV

A re you a girl who consistently uses words that are pleasing to God? Hopefully so. If you genuinely desire to be a good person, your words and your actions must demonstrate your faithfulness to the Creator.

Of course you must never take the Lord's name in vain, but it doesn't stop there. You must also try to speak words of encouragement, words that lift others up, words that give honor to your Heavenly Father.

The Bible clearly warns that you will be judged by the words you speak, so choose those words carefully. And remember this: God is always listening.

Pet Facts: Plenty of Pooches in Paris

It has been estimated that there are more dogs in Paris than people.

THE RIGHT PATH

Now that you are obedient children of God do not live as you did in the past. You did not understand, so you did the evil things you wanted. But be holy in all you do, just as God, the One who called you, is holy.

1 Peter 1:14-15 NCV

How will you respond to Christ's love? Will you take up His cross and follow Him, or will you choose another path? When you place your hopes squarely at the foot of the cross, when you place Jesus squarely at the center of your life, you will be blessed.

The 19th-century writer Hannah Whitall Smith observed, "The crucial question for each of us is this: What do you think of Jesus, and do you yet have a personal acquaintance with Him?" Indeed, the answer to that question determines the quality, the course, and the direction of our lives today and for all eternity.

Let us put down our old ways and pick up His cross. Let us walk the path that He walked.

God's Amazing Animals: Baby Rabbits Look Funny

Rabbits are born with their eyes closed and without fur. But before long, they're looking around and hopping around.

LIFETIME LEARNING

Above all and before all, do this: Get Wisdom! Write this at the top of your list: Get Understanding!

Proverbs 4:7 MSG

Even if you're a very bright young woman, you've still got lots to learn. Even if you're a very wise person, God isn't finished with you yet. Why? Because lifetime learning is part of God's plan—and He certainly hasn't finished teaching you some very important lessons.

Do you seek to live a life of righteousness and wisdom? If so, you must continue to study the ultimate source of wisdom: the Word of God. You must associate, day in and day out, with godly men and women. And, you must act in accordance with your beliefs. When you study God's Word and live according to His commandments, you will become wise . . . and you will be a blessing to your friends, to your family, and to the world.

Pet Facts: People Like Labs!

The most popular dog breed in America is the labrador retriever.

HABITS THAT ARE PLEASING TO GOD

I, the Lord, examine the mind, I test the heart to give to each according to his way, according to what his actions deserve.

Jeremiah 17:10 HCSB

It's an old saying and a true one: First, you make your habits, and then your habits make you. Some habits will inevitably bring you closer to God; other habits will lead you away from the path He has chosen for you. If you sincerely desire to improve your spiritual health, you must honestly examine the habits that make up the fabric of your day. And you must abandon those habits that are displeasing to God.

If you trust God, and if you keep asking for His help, He can transform your life. If you sincerely ask Him to help you, the same God who created the universe will help you defeat the harmful habits that have heretofore defeated you. So, if at first you don't succeed, keep praying. God is listening, and He's ready to help you become a better person if you ask Him . . . so ask today.

Pet Facts: Dog Show History

The first dog show was held in England in 1859. America's biggest dog show, the Westminster show in New York, was first held in 1877.

FOLLOWING HIS FOOTSTEPS

But whoever keeps His word, truly in him the love of God is perfected. This is how we know we are in Him: the one who says he remains in Him should walk just as He walked.

1 John 2:5-6 HCSB

Life is a series of decisions. Each day, we make countless decisions that can bring us closer to God . . . or not. Do you seek to walk in the footsteps of the One from Galilee, or will you choose another path? If you sincerely seek God's peace and His blessings, then you must strive to imitate God's Son.

Thomas Brooks spoke for believers of every generation when he observed, "Christ is the sun, and all the watches of our lives should be set by the dial of his motion." Christ, indeed, is the ultimate Savior of mankind and the personal Savior of those who believe in Him. As His servants, we should walk in His footsteps as we share His love and His message with a world that needs both.

God's Amazing Animals:
Whales Are Natural-born Singers!

Whales love to sing! They use their songs to talk to other whales, or just to entertain themselves.

AIMING HIGH

I can do everything through him that gives me strength.

Philippians 4:13 NIV

Are you willing to dream big dreams? Hopefully so; after all, God promises that we can do "all things" through Him. Yet most of us, even the most devout among us, live far below our potential. We take half measures; we dream small dreams; we waste precious time and energy on the distractions of the world. But God has other plans for us. Our Creator intends that we live faithfully, hopefully, courageously, and abundantly. He knows that we are capable of so much more; and He wants us to do the things we're capable of doing; and He wants us to start doing those things now.

Allow your dreams a place in your prayers and plans. God-given dreams can help you move into the future He is preparing for you.

Barbara Johnson

God's Amazing Animals: About Squirrels

Squirrels are born blind. They eat mostly nuts, fruits, and seeds.

THE SOURCE OF STRENGTH

Happy are the people whose strength is in You, whose hearts are set on pilgrimage.

Psalm 84:5 HCSB

Have you "tapped in" to the power of God? Have you turned your life and your heart over to Him, or are you muddling along under your own power? The answer to this question will determine the quality of your life here on earth and the destiny of your life throughout all eternity.

The Bible tells us that we can do all things through the power of our risen Savior, Jesus Christ. But what does the Bible say about our powers outside the will of Christ? The Bible teaches us that "the wages of sin is death" (Romans 6:23). Our challenge, then, is clear: we must place Christ where He belongs: at the very center of our lives. When we do so, we will surely discover that He offers us the strength to live victoriously in this world and eternally in the next.

Pet Facts: The Long Friendship Between People and Dogs

People and dogs have been friends for a long time. In fact, dogs were the first pets domesticated by people.

THE SEARCH FOR TRUTH

You will know the truth, and the truth will set you free.

John 8:32 HCSB

The words of John 8:32 are both familiar and profound: the truth, indeed, will make you free. Truth is God's way: He commands His children to live in truth, and He rewards those who follow His commandment. Jesus is the personification of a perfect, liberating truth that offers salvation to mankind.

Are you a girl who genuinely wants to walk with God? Do you seek to feel God's peace? Then you must walk in truth, and you must walk with the Savior. There is simply no other way.

I would rather know the truth than be happy in ignorance. If I cannot have both truth and happiness, give me truth. We'll have a long time to be happy in heaven.

A. W. Tozer

God's Amazing Animals: Cheetahs Are "Purrrrr-fect"

Cheetahs do not roar, as the other big cats do. Instead, they purr.

ENCOURAGING WORDS FOR FAMILY AND FRIENDS

Good people's words will help many others.

Proverbs 10:21 NCV

Life is a team sport, and all of us need occasional pats on the back from our teammates. As Christians, we are called upon to spread the Good News of Christ, and we are also called to spread a message of encouragement and hope to the world.

Whether you realize it or not, many people with whom you come in contact every day are in desperate need of a smile or an encouraging word. The world can be a difficult place, and countless friends and family members may be troubled by the challenges of everyday life. Since you don't always know who needs our help, the best strategy is to try to encourage all the people who cross your path. So today, be a world-class source of encouragement to everyone you meet. Never has the need been greater.

Pet Facts: Toto, I Don't Think We're in Kansas Anymore

In the movie *The Wizard of Oz,* the little dog Toto was a cute, smart, and very talented cairn terrier.

WHEN PEOPLE ARE CRUEL

A kind man benefits himself, but a cruel man brings disaster on himself.

Proverbs 11:17 HCSB

Face it: sometimes people can be cruel. And when people are unkind to you or to your friends, you may be tempted to strike back in anger. Don't do it! Instead, remember that God corrects other people's behaviors in His own way, and He doesn't need your help.

So whether you're at a sporting event or anywhere else, for that matter, stay calm. Even when other people misbehave, don't lash out. God wants you to forgive other people as quickly as possible . . . and that's precisely what you should do.

There's a lot in the world we ought to be very angry about: oppression, injustice, discrimination, and cruelty that mistreats the poor and makes fun of the disabled.

Bill Hybels

God's Amazing Animals: What a Catch That Would Be!

The sturgeon is the largest freshwater fish in the world. A big one can weigh over a ton.

KEEPING UP APPEARANCES

Man does not see what the Lord sees, for man sees what is visible, but the Lord sees the heart.

1 Samuel 16:7 HCSB

The world sees you as you appear to be; God sees you as you really are. He sees your heart, and He understands your intentions. The opinions of others should be relatively unimportant to you; however, God's view of you—His understanding of your actions, your thoughts, and your motivations—should be vitally important.

Few things in life are more futile than "keeping up appearances" in order to impress your friends—yet the media would have you believe otherwise. The media would have you believe that everything depends on the color of your hair, the condition of your wardrobe, and the stuff you have. But nothing could be further from the truth. What is important, of course, is pleasing your Father in heaven. You please Him when your intentions are pure and your actions are just. When you do, you will be blessed today, tomorrow, and forever.

God's Amazing Animals: Are They Elephants or Cows? Actually, They're Both!

Female elephants are called cows. And their babies are called calves.

THE WISDOM OF RIGHTEOUSNESS

As shameful conduct is pleasure for a fool, so wisdom is for a man of understanding.

Proverbs 10:23 HCSB

Are you a radically different person because of your decision to form a personal relationship with Jesus? Has Jesus made a BIG difference in your life, or are you basically the same person you were before you invited Him into your heart? The answer to these questions will determine the quality and the direction of your life.

If you're still doing all the same things you did before you became a Christian, it may be time to take an honest look at the current condition of your faith. Why? Because Jesus doesn't want you to be a run-of-the-mill, follow-the-crowd kind of girl. Jesus wants you to be a "new creation" through Him. And that's exactly what you should want for yourself, too.

God's Amazing Animals:
Lions Take Pride in Their Prides

Lions are the only big cats that live in groups. Those groups are called "prides." Every female within the pride is usually related.

HAPPY THOUGHTS

Those who are pure in their thinking are happy, because they will be with God.

Matthew 5:8 NCV

D o you try to think the kind of thoughts that make you happy, not sad? The Bible says that you should. Do you try to think about things that are true and right? The Bible says that you should.

Do you turn away from bad thoughts—and away from people who misbehave? The Bible says that you should.

The Bible instructs you to guard your thoughts against things that are hurtful or wrong. So remember this: when you turn away from the bad thoughts, you've made a very wise choice.

The moment anxious thoughts invade your mind, go to the Lord in prayer. Look first to God. Then, you will see the cause of your anxiety in a whole new light.

Kay Arthur

Pet Facts: Lots and Lots of Dogs

In total, it is believed that there are about 400 million dogs in the world. That's a lot of wagging tails!

MOVING ON

Bad temper is contagious—don't get infected.

Proverbs 22:25 MSG

Today and every day, make sure that you're a girl who is kind to everybody you meet. When you're kind, you show people what it means to be a Christian. That's how God wants you to behave.

Jesus instructed each of us to treat other people in the same way we would want to be treated if we were in their shoes. So if someone says something to you that isn't very nice, don't get angry and don't pay too much attention. Just forgive that person as quickly as you can, and try to move on . . . as quickly as you can.

We are all fallen creatures and all very hard to live with.

C. S. Lewis

God's Amazing Animals: Is It a Hippo, or an African Water Horse, or Both?

Hippos are found in Africa. The name hippopotamus means "river horse."

DON'T FALL IN LOVE WITH STUFF

Don't love the world's ways. Don't love the world's goods. Love of the world squeezes out love for the Father. Practically everything that goes on in the world—wanting your own way, wanting everything for yourself, wanting to appear important—has nothing to do with the Father. It just isolates you from him. The world and all its wanting, wanting, wanting is on the way out—but whoever does what God wants is set for eternity.

1 John 2:15-17 MSG

We live in the world, but we should not worship it. Our job is to place God first and everything else second. But sometimes, putting God in His rightful place is often difficult. In fact, at every turn, or so it seems, we are tempted to do otherwise.

The world is a noisy, distracting place filled with countless chances to stray from God's will. The world seems to cry, "Worship me with your time, your money, your energy, and your thoughts!" But God commands us to worship Him and Him alone; everything else must be secondary.

Pet Facts: Great State, Great Big Dog

The official state dog of Pennsylvania is the Great Dane.

LESSONS IN PATIENCE

Give all your worries and cares to God, for he cares about what happens to you.

1 Peter 5:6 NLT

Are you anxious for God to work out His game plan for your life? Who isn't? As believers, we all want God to do great things for us and through us, and we want Him to do those things now. But sometimes, God has other plans. Sometimes, God's timetable does not coincide with our own. It's worth noting, however, that God's timetable is always perfect.

The next time you find your patience tested to the limit, remember that the world unfolds according to God's plan, not ours. Sometimes, we must wait patiently, and that's as it should be. After all, think how patient God has been with us.

We must leave it to God to answer our prayers in His own wisest way. Sometimes, we are so impatient and think that God does not answer. God always answers! He never fails! Be still. Abide in Him.

Mrs. Charles E. Cowman

God's Amazing Animals: Some Whales Like Company

Some whales like to swim together in groups. A collection of whales is called a pod.

ACCORDING TO GOD

The counsel of the LORD stands forever, the plans of His heart from generation to generation.

Psalm 33:11 NASB

God's wisdom stands forever. God's Word is a light for every generation. Make it your light as well. Use the Bible as a compass for the next stage of your life's journey. Use it as the yardstick by which your behavior is measured. And as you carefully consult the pages of God's Word, prayerfully ask Him to reveal the wisdom that you need. When you take your concerns to God, He will not turn you away; He will, instead, offer answers that are tested and true. Your job is to ask, to listen, and to trust.

This is my song through endless ages: Jesus led me all the way.

Fanny Crosby

Pet Facts: American Homes Contain Lots of Cats

Over a third of American homes have at least 1 cat. And, of course, some of those homes contain 2, 3, 4, or more cats. What's the "purrrrr-fect" number of cats for your house?

THE GOAL IS TO PLEASE GOD

Our only goal is to please God whether we live here or there, because we must all stand before Christ to be judged.

2 Corinthians 5:9-10 NCV

Rick Warren observed, "Those who follow the crowd usually get lost in it." We know those words to be true, but oftentimes we fail to live by them. Instead of trusting God for guidance, we imitate our friends and suffer the consequences. Instead of seeking to please our Father in heaven, we strive to please our peers, with decidedly mixed results. Instead of doing the right thing, we do the "easy" thing or the "popular" thing. And when we do, we pay a high price for our shortsightedness.

Would you like a time-tested formula for successful living? Here is a simple formula that is proven and true: don't give in to peer pressure. Period.

Instead of getting lost in the crowd, you should find guidance from God. Does this sound too simple? Perhaps it is simple, but it is also the only way to reap all the marvelous riches that God has in store for you.

Pet Facts: The Favorite Dog in Germany Is . . .

Not surprisingly, the favorite dog in Germany is . . . the German shepherd.

YES, JESUS LOVES YOU!

You're blessed when you're content with just who you are—no more, no less. That's the moment you find yourselves proud owners of everything that can't be bought.

Matthew 5:5 MSG

You've probably heard these words many times: "Jesus loves me, this I know." These happy words should remind you of this important fact: Jesus loves you very, very much.

When you invite Jesus into your heart, He will be your friend forever. If you make mistakes, He'll still be your friend. When you aren't perfect, He'll still love you. If you feel sorry or sad, He can help you feel better.

Yes, Jesus loves you . . . and you should love yourself. So the next time you feel sad about yourself . . . or something that you've done . . . remember that Jesus loves you, your family loves you, and you should feel that way, too.

God's Amazing Animals: That's Loud!

At 188 decibels, the whistle of the blue whale is the loudest sound produced by any animal.

GOD IS PERFECT; WE ARE NOT

Since we've compiled this long and sorry record as sinners (both us and them) and proved that we are utterly incapable of living the glorious lives God wills for us, God did it for us. Out of sheer generosity he put us in right standing with himself. A pure gift. He got us out of the mess we're in and restored us to where he always wanted us to be. And he did it by means of Jesus Christ.

Romans 3:23 MSG

I f you're your own worst critic, give it up. After all, God doesn't expect you to be perfect, and if that's okay with Him, then it should be okay with you, too.

When you accepted Christ as your Savior, God accepted you for all eternity. Now, it's your turn to accept yourself. When you do, you'll feel a tremendous weight being lifted from your shoulders. And that's as it should be. After all, only one earthly being ever lived life to perfection, and He was the Son of God. The rest of us have fallen short of God's standard and need to be accepting of our own limitations as well as the limitations of others.

Pet Facts: The Favorite Dog in France Is . . .

The favorite dog in France isn't the French poodle; it's the German shepherd.

THINK ABOUT WHAT'S RIGHT

Keep your eyes focused on what is right. Keep looking straight ahead to what is good.

Proverbs 4:25 ICB

In the Book of Proverbs, King Solomon gave us wonderful advice for living wisely. Solomon said that we should keep our eyes "focused on what is right." In other words, we should do our best to say and do the things that we know are pleasing to God.

The next time you're tempted to say an unkind word or to say something that isn't true, remember the advice of King Solomon. Solomon knew that it's always better to do the right thing, even when it's tempting to do otherwise. So if you know something is wrong, don't do it; instead, do what you know to be right. When you do, you'll be saving yourself a lot of trouble and you'll be obeying the Word of God.

Make God's will the focus of your life day by day. If you seek to please Him and Him alone, you'll find yourself satisfied with life.

Kay Arthur

Pet Facts: Why Meow?

Cats don't like to meow at other cats. They like to save that noise for humans.

HOPE IS CONTAGIOUS

I will lift up my eyes to the hills—From whence comes my help? My help comes from the Lord, Who made heaven and earth.

Psalm 121:1-2 NKJV

The more we trust God, the better. And the more we trust God, the more secure we can feel about the future. Optimism is a gift you give yourself—a way of putting the self-fulfilling prophecy to work for you. So if you find yourself focusing on your fears instead of your faith, it's time to redirect your thoughts.

Hope is contagious, and hope inspired by a strong faith in God is highly contagious. So today, as you talk to friends and family members, be sure to share your hopes, your dreams, and your enthusiasm. Your positive outlook will be almost as big a blessing to them as it is to you.

God's Amazing Animals: That's a Lot of Goats

There are over 210 breeds of goats in the world. And, experts estimate that there are approximately 450 million goats around the world.

GOD'S PERSPECTIVE

He will teach us His ways, and we shall walk in His paths.

Isaiah 2:3 NKJV

The words of Psalm 46:10 remind us to "Be still, and know that I am God" (NKJV). When we do so, we encounter the awesome presence of our loving Heavenly Father, and we are blessed beyond words. But, when we ignore the presence of our Creator, we rob ourselves of His perspective, His peace, and His joy.

Today and every day, set aside a time to be still before God. When you do, you can face the day's complications with the wisdom and the perspective that only He can provide.

When considering the size of your problems, there are two categories that you should never worry about: the problems that are small enough for you to handle, and the ones that aren't too big for God to handle.

Marie T. Freeman

Pet Facts: Dogs Like to Work!

Dogs perform many useful tasks for humans including hunting, farm work, and security as well as assisting people who have physical disabilities.

HELPING TO BEAR THE BURDENS

Carry one another's burdens; in this way you will fulfill the law of Christ.

Galatians 6:2 HCSB

Neighbors. We know that we are instructed to love them, and yet there's so little time . . . and we're so busy. No matter. As Christians, we are instructed to love our neighbors just as we love ourselves. Period.

This very day, you will encounter someone who needs a word of encouragement, or a pat on the back, or a helping hand, or a heartfelt prayer. And, if you don't reach out to that person, who will? And if you don't take the time to understand the needs of your neighbors, who will? So, today, look for a neighbor in need . . . and then do something to help. Father's orders.

God wants us to be more sensitive to the feelings and needs of others and less sensitive to our own feelings and needs.

Joyce Meyer

Pet Facts: How Long Do Ferrets Live?

The average ferret lives to be 6 or 7 years old.

MERCY!

Those who show mercy to others are happy, because God will show mercy to them.

Matthew 5:7 NCV

Are you caught in the quicksand of anger? If so, you are not only disobeying God's Word, you are also wasting your time. The world holds few if any rewards for those who remain angrily focused upon the past. Still, the act of forgiveness is difficult.

If there exists even one person against whom you hold bitter feelings, it's time to forgive. Or, if you are angry with yourself for some past mistake or shortcoming, it's finally time to forgive yourself and move on. Bitterness and regret are not part of God's plan for your life. Forgiveness is.

Bitterness is the price we charge ourselves for being unwilling to forgive.

Marie T. Freeman

Pet Facts: Why Do Dogs Dig?

Dogs dig for lots of reasons: to hide food, to go from one place to another, to explore and just to have some fun.

KEEP THE PEACE

Blessed are the peacemakers, because they will be called sons of God.

Matthew 5:9 HCSB

Sometimes, it's easiest to become angry with the people we love the most. After all, we know that they'll still love us no matter how angry we become. But while it's easy to become angry at home, it's usually wrong.

The next time you're tempted to become angry with a brother, or a sister, or a parent, remember that these are the people who love you more than anybody else! Then, calm down. Because peace is always beautiful, especially when it's peace at your house.

The Golden Rule begins at home.

Marie T. Freeman

Pet Facts: Dog Biscuit History

The "Milk Bone" dog biscuit was invented in 1907. Dogs have been happy ever since!

PRAISE FOR THE FATHER; THANKS FOR HIS BLESSINGS

I will give You thanks with all my heart.

Psalm 138:1 HCSB

Okay, you're probably a very busy girl. Sometimes, you may find yourself rushing from place to place with scarcely a moment to spare. And when you're really busy, you may not take time to praise your Creator. Big mistake.

The Bible makes it clear: it pays to praise God. Worship and praise should be a part of everything you do. Otherwise, you quickly lose perspective as you fall prey to the demands of everyday life.

Do you sincerely want to know God in a more meaningful way? Then praise Him for who He is and for what He has done for you. And please don't wait until Sunday morning—praise Him all day long, every day, for as long as you live . . . and then for all eternity.

The time for universal praise is sure to come some day. Let us begin to do our part now.

Hannah Whitall Smith

Pet Facts: Tell Your Cat What You Think

You should talk to your cat often. Cats love to hear the sound of your voice.

PRAYING TO KNOW GOD

Teach me your ways, O Lord, that I may live according to your truth! Grant me purity of heart, that I may honor you.

Psalm 86:11 NLT

Andrew Murray observed, "Some people pray just to pray, and some people pray to know God." Your job, as a maturing believer, is to pray, not out of habit or obligation, but out of a sincere desire to know your Heavenly Father. Through constant prayers, you should petition God, you should praise Him, and you should seek to discover His unfolding plans for your life.

Today, reach out to the Giver of all blessings. Turn to Him for guidance and for strength. Invite Him into every corner of your day. Ask Him to teach you and to lead you. And remember that no matter what your circumstances, God is never far away; He is here . . . always right here. So pray.

Pet Facts: Parakeets Prefer to Imitate High Voices

Experts say that parakeets are more likely to learn to talk mostly from women and children. Why? Because the birds can mimic higher voices more easily.

STAYING OUT OF TROUBLE

Don't envy bad people; don't even want to be around them. All they think about is causing a disturbance; all they talk about is making trouble.

Proverbs 24:1-2 MSG

One way that you can feel better about yourself is by staying out of trouble. And one way that you can stay out of trouble is by making friends with people who, like you, want to do what's right.

Are your friends the kind of kids who encourage you to behave yourself? If so, you've chosen your friends wisely. But if your friends try to get you in trouble, perhaps it's time to think long and hard about making some new friends.

Whether you know it or not, you're probably going to behave like your friends behave. So pick out friends who make you want to behave better, not worse. When you do, you'll feel better about yourself . . . a whole lot better.

Pet Facts: Cats See Well at Night

Cats have great nighttime vision. They can see things at light levels six times lower than the level of light needed for humans to see.

PERSISTENT PRAYER

Watch therefore, and pray always. . . .

Luke 21:36 NKJV

When we weave the habit of prayer into the very fabric of our days, we invite God to become a partner in every aspect of our lives. When we consult God on an hourly basis, we avail ourselves of His wisdom, His strength, and His love. Today, instead of turning things over in your mind, turn them over to God in prayer. Instead of worrying about your next decision, decide to let God lead the way. Don't limit your prayers to meals or to bedtime. Pray constantly about things great and small. God is listening, and He wants to hear from you. Now.

Don't pray when you feel like it; make an appointment with the King and keep it.

Corrie ten Boom

God's Amazing Animals:
You Can Tell a Tiger by Its Stripes!

A tiger's stripes are like fingerprints—no two animals have exactly the same pattern.

THE RIGHT KIND OF TREASURE

Wherever your treasure is, there your heart and thoughts will also be.

Luke 12:34 NLT

Is God a big priority for you . . . or is He an afterthought? Do you give God your best or what's left? Have you given Christ your heart, your soul, your talents, your time, and your testimony? Or are you giving Him little more than a few hours each Sunday morning?

In the Book of Exodus, God warns that we should place no gods before Him (Exodus 20:3). Yet all too often, we place our Lord in second, third, or fourth place as we worship the gods of pride, money, or personal gratification. When we unwittingly place possessions or relationships above our love for the Creator, we must realign our priorities or suffer the consequences.

Does God rule your heart? Make certain that the honest answer to this question is a resounding yes. In the life of every radical believer, God comes first. And that's precisely the place that He deserves in your heart.

Pet Facts: No Wonder Ferrets Are So Cute!

Ferrets get plenty of beauty rest. In fact, they sleep for about 20 hours every day.

THE SIZE OF YOUR PROBLEMS

Ah Lord GOD! Behold, You have made the heavens and the earth by Your great power and by Your outstretched arm! Nothing is too difficult for You.

Jeremiah 32:17 NASB

Negative thoughts are habit-forming; thankfully, so are positive ones. With practice, you can form the habit of focusing on God's priorities and your possibilities. When you do, you'll soon discover that you will spend less time fretting about your challenges and more time praising God for His gifts.

When you call upon the Lord and prayerfully seek His will, He will give you wisdom and perspective. When you make God's priorities your priorities, He will direct your steps and calm your fears. So today and every day hereafter, pray for a sense of balance and perspective. And remember: no problems are too big for God—and that includes yours.

Pet Facts: Cats Love Their Sleep!

A fifteen-year-old cat has probably spent ten years of its life sleeping.

SOLOMON SAYS . . . BE KIND!

A kind person is doing himself a favor. But a cruel person brings trouble upon himself.

Proverbs 11:17 ICB

In the Book of Proverbs, King Solomon warned that unkind behavior leads only to trouble, but kindness is its own reward. Yet in the busyness and stress of 21st-century life, it's easy to become so wrapped up in the obligations of everyday life that we forget to share kind words and good deeds. After all, none of us is perfect and all of us are struggling to manage our lives as best we can. Sometimes, we're bound to fall short.

The next time you're tempted to say an unkind word, remember Solomon. He was one of the wisest men who ever lived, and he knew that it's always better to be kind. And now, you know it, too.

If we're to love people like we should, our hearts have to be as pleasant toward them as our appearances are. Otherwise, we're living a lie.

Mary Hunt

Pet Facts: Want to Win a Dog Race?

Greyhounds are the fastest dogs of all. They can run at speeds up to 45 mph.

GOD TEACHES US

If you hide your sins, you will not succeed. If you confess and reject them, you will receive mercy.

Proverbs 28:13 NCV

The Bible says that when people make mistakes, God corrects them. And that means that if you make a mistake, God will try to find a way to teach you how to keep from making that same mistake again. God doesn't expect you to be perfect, but He does expect you to learn from your mistakes—NOW!

God's correction is purposeful: He intends to guide us back to Him. When we trust God completely and without reservation, He gives us the strength to meet any challenge, the courage to face any trial, and the wisdom to live in His righteousness and in His peace.

Mature people are not emotionally and spiritually devastated by every mistake they make. They are able to maintain some kind of balance in their lives.

Joyce Meyer

God's Amazing Animals: So Many Sheep, So Few People!

The population of New Zealand is 4 million people and 70 million sheep.

LEARNING FROM THE RIGHT PEOPLE

We have around us many people whose lives tell us what faith means. So let us run the race that is before us and never give up. We should remove from our lives anything that would get in the way and the sin that so easily holds us back.

Hebrews 12:1 NCV

It has been said on many occasions that life is a team sport. So, too, is learning how to live. If we are to become mature believers—and if we seek to discover God's purposes in our everyday lives—we need worthy examples and wise mentors.

Are you walking with the wise? Are you spending time with people you admire? Are you learning how to live from people who know how to live? If you genuinely seek to walk with God, then you will walk with those who walk with Him.

We urgently need people who encourage and inspire us to move toward God and away from the world's enticing pleasures.

Jim Cymbala

Pet Facts: Cats Love to Sleep

On average, a cat will sleep about 16 hours a day. That makes for a lot of cat-dreams!

IN SEARCH OF ANSWERS

You will seek Me and find Me when you search for Me with all your heart.

Jeremiah 29:13 HCSB

You've got questions? God's got answers. And if you'd like to hear from Him, here's precisely what you must do: petition Him with a sincere heart; be still; be patient; and listen. Then, in His own time and in His own fashion, God will answer your questions and give you guidance for the journey ahead.

Today, turn over everything to your Creator. Pray constantly about matters great and small. Seek God's instruction and His direction. And remember: God hears your prayers and answers them. But He won't answer the prayers that you don't get around to praying. So pray early and often. And then wait patiently for answers that are sure to come.

The purpose of all prayer is to find God's will and to make that will our prayer.

Catherine Marshall

God's Amazing Animals: A Barkless Dog!

The basenji, an African wolf dog, is the only dog that cannot bark.

BECOMING A MORE PATIENT PERSON

Be gentle to all, able to teach, patient.

2 Timothy 2:24 NKJV

The Book of Proverbs tells us that patience is a very good thing. But for most of us, patience can also be a very hard thing. After all, we have many things that we want, and we want them NOW! But the Bible tells us that we must learn to wait patiently for the things that God has in store for us.

Are you having trouble being patient? If so, remember that patience takes practice, and lots of it, so keep trying. And if you make a mistake, don't be too upset. After all, if you're going to be a really patient person, you shouldn't just be patient with others, you should also be patient with yourself.

Let me encourage you to continue to wait with faith. God may not perform a miracle, but He is trustworthy to touch you and make you whole where there used to be a hole.

Lisa Whelchel

God's Amazing Animals: How Owls See

Owls see very well at night. And, they are farsighted, which means that they see things far away but they can't see things up close very well.

THE BEST TIME TO BE OBEDIENT

The one who has My commandments and keeps them is the one who loves Me. And the one who loves Me will be loved by My Father. I also will love him and will reveal Myself to him.

John 14:21 HCSB

If you look in a dictionary, you'll see that the word "wisdom" means "using good judgement, and knowing what is true." But there's more: it's not enough just to know what's right; if you really want to become a wise person, you must also do what's right.

When we live obediently—and when we seek the companionship of those who do likewise—we reap the spiritual rewards that God intends for us to enjoy. When we strive to do what's right, God blesses us in ways that we cannot fully understand.

A big part of "doing what's right" is learning to be obedient . . . and the best time to start being a more obedient person is right now! Why? Because it's the wise thing to do.

God's Amazing Animals: About a Frog's Tongue

Frogs use their sticky tongues to catch and swallow food. A frog's tongue is attached to the front of its mouth, enabling it to stick its tongue out much farther.

PROMISES YOU CAN TRUST

Do not be afraid or discouraged. For the LORD your God is with you wherever you go.

Joshua 1:9 NLT

God has made quite a few promises to you, and He intends to keep every single one of them. You will find these promises in a book like no other: the Holy Bible. The Bible is your map for life here on earth and for life in heaven.

God is eternal and unchanging. Before He laid the foundations of our universe, He was a being of infinite power and love, and He will remain so throughout all eternity. His promises never fail and they never grow old. You must trust those promises and share them with your family, with your friends, with your classmates, and with the world . . . starting now . . . and ending never.

We have ample evidence that the Lord is able to guide. The promises cover every imaginable situation. All we need to do is to take the hand he stretches out.

Elisabeth Elliot

Pet Facts: Ferrets Are Amazing Squeezers

A small ferret may be able to squeeze through a hole just over an inch wide.

BUSY WITH OUR THOUGHTS

Make your own attitude that of Christ Jesus.
Philippians 2:5 HCSB

Because we are human, we are always busy with our thoughts. We simply can't help ourselves. Our brains never shut off, and even while we're sleeping, we mull things over in our minds. The question is not if we will think; the question is how will we think and what will we think about.

Today, focus your thoughts on God and His will. And if you're a girl who's been plagued by pessimism and doubt, stop thinking like that! Place your faith in God and give thanks for His blessings. Think optimistically about your world and your life. It's the wise way to use your mind. And besides, since you will always be busy with your thoughts, you might as well make those thoughts pleasing (to God) and helpful (to you and yours).

Pet Facts: Parakeets Are Smart!

Parakeets can be taught to jump from hand to hand, to kiss, and perform tricks like climbing ladders or ringing bells in their cages.

WINNERS ARE COURTEOUS

Now finally, all of you should be like-minded and sympathetic, should love believers, and be compassionate and humble.

1 Peter 3:8 HCSB

As Christians, we are instructed to be courteous and compassionate. As Christians, we are called to be gracious, humble, gentle, and kind. But sometimes, we fall short. Sometimes, amid the busyness and confusion of everyday life, we may neglect to share a kind word or a kind deed. This oversight hurts others, and it hurts us as well.

Today, slow yourself down and be alert for those who need your smile, your kind words, or your helping hand. Make kindness a centerpiece of your dealings with others. They will be blessed, and you will be, too. So make this promise to yourself and keep it: honor Christ by obeying His Golden Rule. He deserves no less. And neither, for that matter, do they.

Pet Facts: Maybe Your Hamster Needs Glasses

Hamsters are color blind. And to make matters worse, hamsters can only see up to six inches in front of them.

WHOM WE SHOULD JUDGE

Stop judging others, and you will not be judged. Stop criticizing others, or it will all come back on you. If you forgive others, you will be forgiven.

Luke 6:37 NLT

Here's something worth thinking about: If you judge other people harshly, God will judge you in the same way. But that's not all (thank goodness!). The Bible also promises that if you forgive other people, you, too, will be forgiven.

Are you sometimes tempted to blame people, criticize people, or judge people? If so, remember this: God is already judging what people do, and He doesn't need—or want—your help. So do yourself and everybody else a big favor: leave those kinds of judgments up to Him.

Christians think they are prosecuting attorneys or judges, when, in reality, God has called all of us to be witnesses.

Warren Wiersbe

Pet Facts: Cats Remember More!

Studies have shown that cats have better memories than dogs, monkeys, or orangutans.

WISDOM FROM THE HEART

But the fruit of the Spirit is love, joy, peace, long-suffering, gentleness, goodness, faith, meekness, temperance: against such there is no law.

Galatians 5:22-23 KJV

When we genuinely open our hearts to God, He speaks to us through a small, still voice within. When He does, we can listen, or not. When we pay careful attention to the Father, He leads us along a path of His choosing, a path that leads to abundance, peace, joy, and eternal life. But when we choose to ignore God, we select a path that is not His, and we must endure the consequences of our shortsightedness.

Today, focus your thoughts and your prayers on the path that God intends for you to take. When you do, your loving Heavenly Father will speak to your heart. When He does, listen carefully . . . and trust Him.

Pet Facts: The Swiss National Dog

The national dog of Switzerland is—you guessed it—the Saint Bernard. Saint Bernards are gentle giants who specialize in rescuing people.

LOOK BEFORE YOU LEAP

An impulsive vow is a trap; later you'll wish you could get out of it.

Proverbs 20:25 MSG

Are you, at times, just a little bit impulsive? Do you sometimes fail to look before you leap? If so, God wants to have a little chat with you.

God's Word is clear: as believers, we are called to lead lives of discipline, diligence, moderation, and maturity. But the world often tempts us to behave otherwise. Everywhere we turn, or so it seems, we are faced with powerful temptations to behave in un-disciplined, ungodly ways.

God's Word instructs us to be disciplined in our thoughts and our actions; God's Word warns us against the dangers of impulsive behavior. As believers in a just God, we should act and react accordingly.

Put the brakes on impulsive behavior before impulsive behavior puts the brakes on you.

Anonymous

God's Amazing Animals: Snow Leopards Can Leap!

Snow leopards have very strong legs indeed. That's why they can leap up to seven times their own body length in a single bound.

HOPES, HOPES, AND MORE HOPES

May the God of hope fill you with all joy and peace as you trust in him, so that you may overflow with hope by the power of the Holy Spirit.

Romans 15:13 NIV

God is steadfast in His willingness to protect us. We, in turn, must be steadfast in our willingness to be protected! In other words, we must willingly accept the protection that flows freely from the unwavering heart of God.

Hope is a very good thing to have . . . and to share. So make this promise to yourself and keep it: promise yourself that you'll be a hopeful person. Think good thoughts. Trust God. Become friends with Jesus. And trust your hopes, not your fears. Then, when you've filled your heart with hope and gladness, share your good thoughts with friends. They'll be better for it, and so will you.

Christ can put a spring in your step and a thrill in your heart. Optimism and cheerfulness are products of knowing Christ.

Billy Graham

Pet Facts: What Do You Call Lots of Kittens?

A bunch of kittens is called a kindle.

PROBLEM-SOLVING 101

People who do what is right may have many problems, but the Lord will solve them all.

Psalm 34:19 NCV

The game of life is an exercise in problem-solving. The question is not whether we will encounter problems; the real question is how we will choose to address them. When it comes to solving the problems of everyday living, we often know precisely what needs to be done, but we may be slow in doing it—especially if what needs to be done is difficult or uncomfortable for us. So we put off till tomorrow what should be done today.

The words of Psalm 34 remind us that the Lord solves problems for "people who do what is right." And usually, doing "what is right" means doing the uncomfortable work of confronting our problems sooner rather than later. So with no further ado, let the problem-solving begin . . . now.

Pet Facts: Parakeets Can Learn Lots of Words

Boy parakeets can learn several hundred words and girl parakeets can learn about a hundred words, sometimes more.

YOUR SHINING LIGHT

You are the light of the world. A city situated on a hill cannot be hidden. No one lights a lamp and puts it under a basket, but rather on a lampstand, and it gives light for all who are in the house. In the same way, let your light shine before men, so that they may see your good works and give glory to your Father in heaven.

Matthew 5:14-16 HCSB

Ask yourself this question: Are you the kind of role model that your friends and classmates should want to copy? If so, congratulations. You're a wise young woman. But if certain aspects of your behavior could stand improvement, the best day to begin your self-improvement regimen is this one.

Whether you realize it or not, people you care about are watching your behavior, and they're learning how to live. You owe it to them—and to yourself—to live wisely, joyfully, righteously, and well.

God's Amazing Animals: What Penguins Like to Eat

Penguins eat fish and other sea life that they catch underwater. Penguins can drink sea water.

GOD'S PERFECT LOVE

This is what real love is: It is not our love for God; it is God's love for us in sending his Son to be the way to take away our sins.

1 John 4:10 NCV

I f God had a refrigerator in heaven, your picture would be on it. And that fact should make you feel very good about the person you are today and the person you can become tomorrow.

God's love for you is bigger and more wonderful than you can imagine. So do this, and do it right now: accept God's amazing love with open arms and welcome His Son Jesus into your heart. When you do, you'll most certainly feel better about yourself . . . and your life will be changed forever.

Love is not something God does; love is something God is.

Beth Moore

Pet Facts: A Dog Hears Things You Can't Hear

Dogs can hear a wider range of sounds than people can. Dogs hear both higher sounds and lower sounds than humans.

SUCCESS ACCORDING TO GOD

Live the way the Lord your God has commanded you so that you may live and have what is good.

Deuteronomy 5:33 NCV

How do you define success? Do you define it as the accumulation of stuff, stuff, and more stuff? If so, you need to reorder your priorities. Genuine success has little to do with fame or fortune; it has everything to do with God's gift of love and with His promise of salvation.

If you have allowed Christ to reign over your life, you are already a towering success in the eyes of God, but there is still more that you can do. Your task—as a believer who has been touched by the Creator's grace—is to accept the spiritual abundance and peace that He offers through the person of His Son. Then, you can share the healing message of God's love and His abundance with a world that desperately needs both. When you do, you have reached the pinnacle of success.

God's Amazing Animals:
A Very Short Tale about a Lion's Tail

Unlike other big cats, lions have a tuft of hair at the end of their tails. The end.

MAKE THEM PROUD

Give generously, for your gifts will return to you later.
Ecclesiastes 11:1 NLT

I t's tempting to be selfish, but it's wrong. It's tempting to want to keep everything for yourself, but it's better to share. It's tempting to say, "No, that's MINE!" but it's better to say, "I'll share it with you."

Are you sometimes tempted to be a little stingy? Are you sometimes tempted to say, "No, I don't want to share that!"—and then do you feel a little sorry that you said it? If that describes you, don't worry: everybody is tempted to be a little bit selfish. Your job is to remember this: even when it's tempting to be selfish, you should try very hard not to be. Because when you're generous, not selfish, you'll make your parents proud and you'll make your Father in heaven proud, too.

Pet Facts: Hamster Homes

In the wild, hamsters line their tunnels with grasses or hair shed from other animals to help maintain a comfy temperature in their burrows (often around 60°F).

TRUSTING THE FUTURE TO GOD

"I say this because I know what I am planning for you," says the Lord. "I have good plans for you, not plans to hurt you. I will give you hope and a good future."

Jeremiah 29:11 NCV

How bright is your future? Well, if you're a faithful believer, God's plans for you are so bright that you'd better wear shades. But here's an important question: How bright do you believe your future to be? Are you expecting a terrific tomorrow, or are you dreading a terrible one? The answer you give will have a powerful impact on the way tomorrow turns out.

Do you trust in the ultimate goodness of God's game plan for your life? You should. After all, God created you for a very important reason: His reason. And you still have important work to do: His work. So today, as you live in the present and look to the future, remember that God has an amazing plan for you. Act—and believe—accordingly.

Pet Facts: Cats Are Great Jumpers

Cats are great athletes! A cat can jump as much as seven times its height.

USING GOD'S GIFTS

God has given gifts to each of you from his great variety of spiritual gifts. Manage them well so that God's generosity can flow through you.

1 Peter 4:10 NLT

The gifts that you possess are gifts from the Giver of all things good. Do you have a spiritual gift? Share it. Do you have a testimony about the things that Christ has done for you? Don't leave your story untold. Do you possess financial resources? Share them. Do you have particular talents? Hone your skills and use them for God's glory.

When you obey God by sharing His gifts freely and without fanfare, you invite Him to bless you more and more. Today, be a faithful steward of your talents and treasures. And then prepare yourself for even greater blessings that are sure to come.

Pet Facts: Gerbils Like to Pound the Ground!

"Thumping" is an interesting gerbil behavior. Gerbils often pound both hind legs on the ground when they are excited or stressed.

YOUR PARTNERSHIP WITH GOD

God is working in you to help you want to do and be able to do what pleases him.

Philippians 2:13 NCV

You are God's work-in-progress. God wants to mold your heart and guide your path, but because He created you as a creature of free will, He will not force you to become His. That choice is yours alone, and it is a choice that should be reflected in every decision you make and every step you take.

Today, as you encounter the challenges of everyday life, strengthen your partnership with God through prayer, through obedience, through praise, through thanksgiving, and through service. God is the ultimate partner, and He wants to be your partner in every aspect of your life. Please don't turn Him down.

Every experience God gives us, every person he puts in our lives, is the perfect preparation for the future that only he can see.

Corrie ten Boom

Pet Facts: A Cat's Life

On average, cats live to be about 12 to 15 years old.

GUARD YOUR THOUGHTS

Be careful what you think, because your thoughts run your life.

Proverbs 4:23 NCV

Do you try to think good thoughts about your friends, your family, your teammates, your opponents, and yourself? The Bible says that you should. Do you lift your hopes and your prayers to God many times each day? The Bible says that you should. Do you say "no" to people who want you to do bad things or think bad thoughts? The Bible says that you should.

The Bible teaches you to guard your thoughts against things that are hurtful or wrong. So remember this: When you turn away from bad thoughts and turn instead toward God and His Son Jesus, you will be protected . . . and you will be blessed.

Attitude is the mind's paintbrush; it can color any situation.

Barbara Johnson

God's Amazing Animals: High Jumpers

Kangaroos have very powerful legs, and they can jump very high. In fact, kangaroos can sometimes jump three times their own height.

FINISHING YOUR WORK

It is better to finish something than to start it. It is better to be patient than to be proud.

Ecclesiastes 7:8 NCV

As you travel through life, you will undoubtedly experience your fair share of disappointments, detours, and false starts. When you do, don't become discouraged: God's not finished with you yet.

The old saying is as true today as it was when it was first spoken: "Life is a marathon, not a sprint." That's why wise travelers select a traveling companion who never tires and never falters. That partner, of course, is your Heavenly Father.

Are you tired? Ask God for strength. Are you discouraged? Believe in His promises. Are you defeated? Pray as if everything depended upon God, and work as if everything depended upon you. And finally, have faith that you play an important role in God's great plan for mankind—because you do.

God's Amazing Animals:
The Giant Panda Starts Out as a Very Tiny Baby

A giant panda cub weighs only about 5 ounces at birth. That's about the same as a juice box.

AN HONEST HEART

In every way be an example of doing good deeds. When you teach, do it with honesty and seriousness.

Titus 2:7 NCV

Where does honesty begin? In your own heart and your own head. If you sincerely want to be an honest person, then you must ask God to help you find the courage to be honest all of the time.

Honesty is not a "sometimes" thing. If you intend to be a truthful person, you must make truthfulness a habit that becomes so much a part of you that you don't have to decide whether or not you're going to tell the truth. Instead, you will simply tell the truth because it's who you are.

Lying is an easy habit to fall into, and a terrible one. So make up your mind that you're going to be an honest person, and then stick to your decision. That's what your parents want you to do, and that's what God wants, too. And since they love you more than you know, trust them. And always tell the truth.

Pet Facts: They're Very Sound Sleepers!

Ferrets can sleep so soundly that they cannot be woken up even when picked up and jostled.

GREAT WORKS

I assure you: The one who believes in Me will also do the works that I do. And he will do even greater works than these, because I am going to the Father.

John 14:12 HCSB

Make no mistake about it: You and Jesus, working together, can do miraculous things. In fact, miraculous things are exactly what Christ intends for you to do, but He won't force you to do great things on His behalf. The decision to become a full-fledged participant in His power is a decision that you must make for yourself.

The words of John 14:12 make this promise: when you put absolute faith in Christ, you can share in His power. Today, trust the Savior's promise and expect a miracle in His name.

Our Lord does not care so much for the importance of our works as for the love with which they are done.

St. Teresa of Avila

Pet Facts: Pets Make You Happy

A survey found that nine out of ten pet owners said their animal makes them smile more than once a day.

WHY AM I HERE?

May He give you what your heart desires and fulfill your whole purpose.

Psalm 20:4 HCSB

"Why did God put me here?" It's an easy question to ask and, at times, a very difficult question to answer.

Are you earnestly trying to figure out what God wants you to do next? If so, ask Him sincerely, prayerfully, and often. When you do, God will help you find a worthy purpose for your life. Plus, you'll experience abundance, peace, joy, and power—God's power. And that's the only kind of power that really matters.

God created you for a reason; He has important work for you to do; and He's waiting patiently for you to do it. And the next step is up to you.

If the Lord calls you, He will equip you for the task He wants you to fulfill.

Warren Wiersbe

God's Amazing Animals: Jaguars Are Big Cats

The jaguar is the biggest cat native to North America. Fully grown, it can weigh almost 300 pounds!

WINNING AND LOSING

Thanks be to God! He gives us the victory through our Lord Jesus Christ. Therefore, my dear brothers, stand firm. Let nothing move you. Always give yourselves fully to the work of the Lord, because you know that your labor in the Lord is not in vain.

1 Corinthians 15:57-58 NIV

In our competitive world, it's easy to start believing that winning is all important. But, of course, it's not. And, of course, it's easy to start believing that losing is disastrous. But, once again, it's not.

When it comes to winning and losing, you should be far more concerned with winning God's approval than with winning anything else. So please keep winning and losing in perspective. And be sure you're focused on God first, nothing else. If you're a winner according to God's rules, you're a winner, period. And nothing can ever change that.

Pet Facts: Hamsters Are Smarter Than You Think

Hamsters can remember their relatives. And, hamsters can be taught how to recognize their own names. Who says rodents aren't smart?

FAITH ABOVE FEELINGS

Now the just shall live by faith.

Hebrews 10:38 NKJV

Hebrews 10:38 teaches that we should live by faith. Yet sometimes, despite our best intentions, negative feelings can rob us of the peace that would otherwise be ours through Christ. When anger or fear separates us from the spiritual blessings that God has in store, we must rethink our priorities and renew our faith. And we must place faith above feelings.

Human emotions are highly variable, decidedly unpredictable, and often unreliable. Our emotions are like the weather, only far more fickle. So we must learn to live by faith, not by the ups and downs of our own emotional roller coasters.

Sometime during this day, you will probably be gripped by a strong negative emotion. Distrust it. Reign it in. Test it. And turn it over to God. Your emotions will inevitably change; God will not. So trust Him completely as you watch your feelings slowly evaporate into thin air—which, of course, they will.

God's Amazing Animals: Elephants Are Very Big!

Elephants are the largest land-dwelling animals in the world.

REAL WINNERS AREN'T ENVIOUS

Let us not become boastful, challenging one another, envying one another.

Galatians 5:26 NASB

God's Word warns us that envy is sin. So, we must guard ourselves against the natural tendency to feel resentment and jealousy when other people experience good fortune.

As believers, we have absolutely no reason to be envious of any people on earth. After all, as Christians we are already recipients of the greatest gift in all creation: God's grace. We have been promised the gift of eternal life through God's only begotten Son, and we must count that gift as our most precious possession.

Rather than succumbing to the sin of envy, we should focus on the marvelous things that God has done for us—starting with Christ's sacrifice. And we must refrain from preoccupying ourselves with the blessings that God has chosen to give others.

So here's a surefire formula for a happier, healthier life: Count your own blessings and let your neighbors count theirs. It's the godly way to live.

Pet Facts: How Long Do Parakeets Live?

Parakeets can live to be 15 years old, sometimes older.

FOCUS ON THE RIGHT THINGS

Keep your eyes focused on what is right, and look straight ahead to what is good.

Proverbs 4:25 NCV

Where does a good attitude begin? It starts in our hearts and works its way out from there. Jesus taught us that a pure heart is a wonderful blessing. It's up to each of us to fill our hearts with love for God, love for Jesus, and love for all people. When we do, good things happen.

Sometimes, of course, we don't feel much like feeling good. Sometimes, when we're tired, or frustrated, or angry, we simply don't want to have a good attitude. On those days when we're feeling bad, it's time to calm down . . . and rest up.

Do you want to be the best person you can be? Then you shouldn't grow tired of doing the right things . . . and you shouldn't ever grow tired of thinking the right thoughts.

Holiness is not the way to Jesus—Jesus is the way to holiness.

Anonymous

Pet Facts: Dogs Hear Better

Dog have far better hearing than people. Dogs can hear sounds four times farther away than humans.

THE ULTIMATE ARMOR

Finally, be strong in the Lord and in his mighty power. Put on the full armor of God so that you can take your stand against the devil's schemes.

Ephesians 6:10-11 NIV

In a world filled with dangers and temptations, God is the ultimate armor. In a world filled with misleading messages, God's Word is the ultimate truth. In a world filled with more frustrations than we can count, God's Son offers the ultimate peace. Will you accept God's peace and wear God's armor against the dangers of our world? Hopefully so.

Sometimes, in the crush of everyday life, God may seem far away, but He is not. God is everywhere you have ever been and everywhere you will ever go. He is with you night and day; He knows your thoughts and your prayers. His is your ultimate Protector. And, when you earnestly seek His protection, you will find it because He is here—always—waiting patiently for you to reach out to Him.

Pet Facts: A Fat Cat!

The heaviest domestic cat on record weighed almost 47 pounds.

TRUST HIM

Trust the Lord with all your heart, and don't depend on your own understanding. Remember the Lord in all you do, and he will give you success.

Proverbs 3:5-6 NCV

Sometimes, things happen that we simply don't understand. But God does. And He has a reason for everything that He does.

God doesn't explain Himself in ways that we can easily comprehend. So here's what we should do: instead of trying to understanding every aspect of God's unfolding plan for our lives and our world, we must be satisfied to trust Him completely. We cannot know God's motivations, nor can we understand His actions. We can, however, trust Him, and we must.

God is God. He knows what he is doing. When you can't trace his hand, trust his heart.

Max Lucado

Pet Facts: Dogs Like Company

Most dogs don't like to be left alone so they bark or howl. If you want to make your dog feel more comfortable while you're away, you might want to leave the radio or television on.

PLEASING GOD!

For am I now trying to win the favor of people, or God? Or am I striving to please people? If I were still trying to please people, I would not be a slave of Christ.

Galatians 1:10 HCSB

Are you a people-pleaser or a God-pleaser? Hopefully, you're far more concerned with pleasing God than you are with pleasing your friends. But face facts: even if you're a devoted Christian, you're still going to feel the urge to impress your friends—and sometimes that urge will be strong.

Today offers you a fresh start, a brand new chance to follow God's game plan. So here's the choice you face: you can choose to please God first, or you can fall victim to peer pressure. That choice is yours—and so are the consequences.

Joy and victory come from allowing Christ to do "the hard thing" with us.

Beth Moore

God's Amazing Animals: And This Final Word . . .

The last animal in the dictionary is the zyzzyva, a tropical American weevil that is often harmful to plants.

A POWER BEYOND UNDERSTANDING

I pray also that you will have greater understanding in your heart so you will know the hope to which he has called us and that you will know how rich and glorious are the blessings God has promised his holy people. And you will know that God's power is very great for us who believe.

Ephesians 1:18-19 NCV

Ours is a God of infinite possibilities. But sometimes, because of limited faith and limited understanding, we wrongly assume that God cannot or will not intervene in our lives. Such assumptions are simply wrong.

Are you afraid to ask God to do big things in your life? Is your faith threadbare and worn? If so, it's time to abandon your doubts and reclaim your faith in God's promises.

God's Holy Word makes it clear: absolutely nothing is impossible for the Lord. And since the Bible means what it says, you can be comforted in the knowledge that the Creator of the universe can do miraculous things in your own life and in the lives of your loved ones. Your challenge, as a believer, is to take God at His word, and to expect the miraculous.

Pet Facts: Gerbils Like Company

Gerbils, being highly social animals, live best in pairs.

YOU FEEL BETTER ABOUT YOURSELF WHEN YOU SHARE

Be generous to the poor—you'll never go hungry; shut your eyes to their needs, and run a gauntlet of curses.

Proverbs 28:27 MSG

Whether you're playing a team sport or doing just about anything else, it's good to be unselfish. And the same thing applies when you play the game of life.

The more you share, the quicker you'll discover this fact: Good things happen to people (like you) who are kind enough to share the blessings that God has given them. Sharing makes you feel better about yourself. Remember that the best rewards go to the kids who are kind and generous—not to the people who are unkind or stingy. So do what's right: share. You'll feel lots better about yourself when you do.

God's Amazing Animals: That's a Big Wing Span

The albatross has a wing span of up to 14 feet and only needs to visit land once every few years. Amazingly, these birds can travel hundreds of thousands of miles without ever touching land.

A FAITH BIGGER THAN FEAR

Do not let your hearts be troubled. Trust in God; trust also in me. In my Father's house are many rooms; if it were not so, I would have told you. I am going there to prepare a place for you.

John 14:1-2 NIV

American clergyman Edward Everett Hale observed, "Some people bear three kinds of trouble—the ones they've had, the ones they have, and the ones they expect to have." How true. But a better strategy for you is this: accept the past, live in the present, and place the future in God's capable hands.

As you face the challenges of everyday life, you may be comforted by this fact: Trouble, of every kind, is temporary. And worries, of every kind, are temporary. But God's love is everlasting. The troubles that concern you will pass. God remains. And with these thoughts in mind, it's now time for you to place today's challenges in their proper perspective.

Pet Facts: How Do You Make a Ferret Happy?

By giving it a small place to crawl into. Ferrets like small dark spaces to sleep.

GENTLE WORDS

Always be humble, gentle, and patient, accepting each other in love.

Ephesians 4:2 NCV

The Bible tells us that gentle words are helpful and that cruel words are not. But sometimes, especially when we're angry or frustrated, our words and our actions may not be so gentle. Sometimes, we may say things or do things that are unkind or hurtful to others. When we do, we're wrong.

So the next time you're tempted to strike out in anger, don't. And if you want to help your family and friends, remember that gentle words are better than harsh words and good deeds are better than the other kind. Always!

A little kindly advice is better than a great deal of scolding.

Fanny Crosby

Pet Facts: What Do You Call a Hamster?

A girl hamster is called a sow, a boy hamster is a boar, and a baby hamster is called a pup.

YOUR FAMILY HAS RULES

This is how we are sure that we have come to know Him: by keeping His commands.

1 John 2:3 HCSB

Face facts: your family has rules . . . rules that you're not supposed to break.

If you're old enough to know right from wrong, then you're old enough to do something about it. In other words, you should always try to obey your family's rules.

How can you tell "the right thing" from "the wrong thing"? By listening carefully to your parents, that's how.

The more self-control you have, the easier it is to obey your parents. Why? Because, when you learn to think first and do things next, you avoid making silly mistakes. So here's what you should do: First, slow down long enough to listen to your parents. Then, do the things that you know your parents want you to do.

Face facts: your family has rules . . . and it's better for everybody when you obey them.

God's Amazing Animals: Blue Lobster? Not Likely!

One in 5,000 North Atlantic lobsters are born bright blue.

THE COURAGE TO FOLLOW GOD

Be strong and courageous, and do the work. Don't be afraid or discouraged, for the Lord God, my God, is with you. He won't leave you or forsake you.

1 Chronicles 28:20 HCSB

Because we are saved by a risen Christ, we can have hope for the future, no matter how tough our circumstances may seem. After all, God has promised that we are His throughout eternity. And, He has told us that we must place our hopes in Him.

Today, summon the courage to follow God. Even if the path seems difficult, even if your heart is fearful, trust your Heavenly Father and follow Him. Trust Him with your day and your life. Do His work, care for His children, and share His Good News. Let Him guide your steps. He will not lead you astray.

Pet Facts: Who Invented the Cat Door?

Sir Isaac Newton discovered gravity and invented calculus, but that's not all. He also invented the cat door.

STARTING YOUR DAY

It is good to give thanks to the Lord, to sing praises to the Most High. It is good to proclaim your unfailing love in the morning, your faithfulness in the evening.

Psalm 92:1-2 NLT

How do you begin your day? Do you sleep until the last possible moment, giving yourself barely enough time to grab your things and rush out the door without giving a single thought to God? Hopefully, that's not the case. If you're smart, you'll start your day with a prayer of thanks to your Heavenly Father.

Each new day is a gift from God, and if you're determined to be a wise young woman, you'll spend a few quiet moments thanking the Giver. It's the very best way to start your day.

As we spend time reading, applying, and obeying our Bibles, the Spirit of Truth who is also the Spirit of Jesus increasingly reveals Jesus to us.

Anne Graham Lotz

Pet Facts: People Prefer Persians

The most popular cat breed in America is the Persian.

A HEALTHY FEAR

Reverence for the Lord is the foundation of true wisdom. The rewards of wisdom come to all who obey him.

Psalm 111:10 NLT

The Bible instructs us that a healthy fear of the Lord is the foundation of wisdom. Yet sometimes, in our shortsightedness, we fail to show respect for our Creator because we fail to obey Him. When we do, our disobedience always has consequences, and sometimes those consequences are severe.

When we honor the Father by obeying His commandments, we receive His love and His grace. Today, let us demonstrate our respect for God by developing a healthy fear of disobeying Him.

A healthy fear of God will do much to deter us from sin.

Charles Swindoll

Pet Facts: What Does a Parrot Really Look Like?

Parrots have curved beaks, strong legs, and webbed feet. They are often brightly colored, and they are considered to be among the most popular birds on planet earth.

WINNERS ARE ENTHUSIASTIC

Do your work with enthusiasm. Work as if you were serving the Lord, not as if you were serving only men and women.

Ephesians 6:7 NCV

D o you see each day as a glorious opportunity to serve God and follow His game plan? Are you enthused about life, or do you struggle through each day giving scarcely a thought to God's blessings? Are you constantly praising God for His gifts, and are you sharing His Good News with the world? And are you excited about the possibilities for service that God has placed before you, whether at home, at work, at church, or at school? You should be.

You are the recipient of Christ's sacrificial love. Accept it enthusiastically and share it fervently. Jesus deserves your enthusiasm; the world deserves it; and you deserve the experience of sharing it.

God's Amazing Animals:
That's a Whole Lot of Bugs!

It has been estimated that for every person on earth, there are perhaps as many as 200 million insects.

USING OUR GIFTS

I remind you to keep using the gift God gave you . . . .
Now let it grow, as a small flame grows into a fire.

2 Timothy 1:6 NCV

Face it: you've got an array of talents that need to be refined. All people possess special gifts—bestowed from the Father above—and you are no exception. But, your particular gift is no guarantee of success; it must be cultivated—by you—or it will go unused . . . and God's gift to you will be squandered.

Are you willing to do the hard work that's required to discover your talents and to develop them? If you are wise, you'll answer "yes." After all, if you don't make the most of your talents, who has the most to lose? You do!

So make a promise to yourself that you will earnestly seek to discover the talents that God has given you. Then, nourish those talents and make them grow. Finally, vow to share your gifts with the world for as long as God gives you the power to do so. After all, the best way to say "Thank You" for God's gifts is to use them.

Pet Facts: A Dog with Duck Feet?

Newfoundland dogs are strong swimmers, in part, because they have webbed feet.

WORKING TOGETHER

Work at getting along with each other and with God. Otherwise you'll never get so much as a glimpse of God.

Hebrews 12:14 MSG

Teamwork works. And helping other people can be fun! When you help others, you feel better about yourself—and you'll know that God approves of what you're doing.

When you learn how to cooperate with your family and teammates, you'll soon discover that it's more fun when everybody works together.

So do your teammates and your family members a favor: learn better ways to share and better ways to cooperate. It's the right thing to do and the best way to build a winning team.

The best times in life are made a thousand times better when shared with a dear friend.

Luci Swindoll

Pet Facts: St. Bernards Are Big!

The St. Bernard is the heaviest dog. A fully-grown St. Bernard can weigh 200 pounds, or more. So don't try to pick one up by yourself!

THOUGHTFUL WORDS

The wise don't tell everything they know, but the foolish talk too much and are ruined.

Proverbs 10:14 NCV

Think . . . pause . . . then speak: How wise is the person who can communicate in this way. But all too often, in the rush to have ourselves heard, we speak first and think next . . . with unfortunate results.

God's Word reminds us that, "Reckless words pierce like a sword, but the tongue of the wise brings healing" (Proverbs 12:18 NIV). If we seek to be a source of encouragement to friends and family, then we must measure our words carefully. Words are important: they can hurt or heal. Words can uplift us or discourage us, and reckless words, spoken in haste, cannot be erased.

Today, seek to encourage everybody you meet. Measure your words carefully. Speak wisely, not impulsively. Remember that you have the power to heal others or to injure them, to lift others up or to hold them back. When you lift them up, your wisdom will bring healing and comfort to a world that needs both.

Pet Facts: How Long Does a Gerbil Live?

On average, a gerbil lives to be 2 or 3 years old.

POPULARITY CONTESTS

Do you think I am trying to make people accept me? No, God is the One I am trying to please. Am I trying to please people? If I still wanted to please people, I would not be a servant of Christ.

Galatians 1:10 NCV

If you're like most people, you seek the admiration of your neighbors, your teammates, and your family members. But the eagerness to please others should never overshadow your eagerness to please God. In every aspect of your life, pleasing your Heavenly Father should come first.

Would you like a time-tested formula for successful living? Here is a formula that is proven and true: Seek God's approval first and other people's approval later. Does this sound too simple? Perhaps it is simple, but it is also the only way to reap the marvelous riches that God has in store for you.

God's Amazing Animals:
Ducks Don't Mind Cold Weather

Ducks are comfortable walking on ice and swimming in icy water because their feet are unable to feel cold.

SELF-DEFEATING ANGER

When you are angry, do not sin, and be sure to stop being angry before the end of the day. Do not give the devil a way to defeat you.

Ephesians 4:26–27 NCV

In the game of life, anger is an emotion that can be dangerous and counterproductive. In fact, when you allow yourself to become angry, you are certain to defeat at least one person: yourself. When you allow the minor frustrations of everyday life to hijack your emotions, you do harm to yourself, to your friends, and to your family. So today and every day, guard yourself against the kind of angry thinking that inevitably takes a toll on your emotions and your relationships.

Life is too short to spend it being angry.

Barbara Johnson

Pet Facts: What Parrots Like to Eat

Most parrots prefer seeds, but some parrots prefer fruit, nectar, flowers, or small insects.

SLOW DOWN

You can't go wrong when you love others. When you add up everything in the law code, the sum total is love. But make sure that you don't get so absorbed and exhausted in taking care of all your day-by-day obligations that you lose track of the time and doze off, oblivious to God.

Romans 13:10-11 MSG

Sure you're a very busy girl. But here's a question: are you able to squeeze time into your hectic schedule for God? Hopefully so! But if you're one of those who rush through the day with scarcely a single moment to talk with your Creator, it's time to reshuffle your priorities.

You live in a noisy world filled with distractions, frustrations, temptations, and complications. But if you allow the distractions of everyday life to distract you from God's peace, you're doing yourself a big disservice. Nothing is more important than the time you spend with your Heavenly Father. So here's some good advice: instead of rushing nonstop through the day, slow yourself down long enough to have a few quiet minutes with God.

Pet Facts: That's Quite a Long Swim ... For a Bear!

Polar bears can swim up to 60 miles without pausing for a rest.

THE DANGERS OF PRIDE

Pride leads only to shame; it is wise to be humble.

Proverbs 11:2 NCV

The words from Proverbs 11 remind us that pride and destruction are traveling partners. But as imperfect human beings, we are tempted to puff out our chests and crow about our own accomplishments. Big mistake.

As Christians, we have a profound reason to be humble: We have been refashioned and saved by Jesus Christ, and that salvation came not because of our own good works but because of God's grace. Thus, we are not "self-made"; we are "God-made" and "Christ-saved." How, then, can we be boastful? The answer, of course, is simple: if we are honest with ourselves and with our God, we cannot be boastful. In the quiet moments, when we search the depths of our own hearts, we know that whatever "it" is, God did that. And He deserves the credit.

The Lord sends no one away empty except those who are full of themselves.

D. L. Moody

God's Amazing Animals: How to Recognize a Barn Owl

Barn owls can be recognized by their heart shaped face.

FORGIVE ONE ANOTHER

Be gentle with one another, sensitive. Forgive one another as quickly and thoroughly as God in Christ forgave you.

Ephesians 4:32 MSG

Are you the kind of girl who has a tough time forgiving and forgetting? If so, welcome to the club. Most of us find it difficult to forgive the people who have hurt us. And that's too bad because life would be much simpler if we could forgive people "once and for all" and be done with it. Yet forgiveness is seldom that easy. Usually, the decision to forgive is straightforward, but the process of forgiving is more difficult. Forgiveness is a journey that requires effort, time, perseverance, and prayer.

If you sincerely wish to forgive someone, pray for that person. And then pray for yourself by asking God to heal your heart. Don't expect forgiveness to be easy or quick, but rest assured: with God as your partner, you can forgive . . . and you will.

Pet Facts: Danes and Wolfhounds Are Very Tall Dogs!

The tallest dogs are the Great Dane and the Irish wolfhound. They are up to three feet tall at the shoulder, and sometimes even taller than that.

DOING THE RIGHT THING

Do what is right and good in the Lord's sight, so that you may prosper and so that you may enter and possess the good land the Lord your God swore to [give] your fathers.

Deuteronomy 6:18 HCSB

Oswald Chambers advised, "Never support an experience which does not have God as its source, and faith in God as its result." These words serve as a powerful reminder that, as Christians, we are called to walk with God and obey His commandments. But, we live in a world that presents us with countless temptations to stray far from God's path. We Christians, when confronted with sin, have clear instructions: Walk—or better yet run—in the opposite direction.

Today, take every step of your journey with God as your traveling companion. Read His Word and follow His commandments. Support only those activities that enhance your spiritual growth. Be an example of righteous living to your friends, to your neighbors, and to your family. Then, reap the blessings that God has promised to all those who live according to His will and His Word.

Pet Facts: Where Did Gerbils First Come From?

Believe it or not, the common pet gerbil originated in Mongolia.

CHOICES MATTER

But Daniel purposed in his heart that he would not defile himself....

Daniel 1:8 KJV

Your life is a series of choices. From the instant you wake up in the morning until the moment you nod off to sleep at night, you make lots of decisions: decisions about the things you do, decisions about the words you speak, and decisions about the thoughts you choose to think. Simply put, the quality of those decisions determines the quality of your life.

So, if you sincerely want to lead a life that is pleasing to God, you must make choices that are pleasing to Him. And you know what? He deserves no less . . . and neither, for that matter, do you.

Choices can change our lives profoundly.

Gloria Gaither

Pet Facts: When Puppies See the Light

Puppies are born with their eyes closed. About 12 to 15 days after they're born, puppies open their eyes, and the fun really begins!

YOUR ATTITUDE

Make your own attitude that of Christ Jesus.

Philippians 2:5 HCSB

Your attitude can make you happy or sad, grumpy or glad, joyful or mad. And, your attitude doesn't just control the way that you think; it also controls how you behave. If you have a good attitude, you'll behave well. And if you have a bad attitude, you're more likely to mess up.

Have you spent any time thinking about the way that you think? Do you pay much attention to your attitude? Hopefully so! After all, a good attitude is better than a bad one . . . lots better.

You have more control over your attitude than you think. So do your best to make your attitude a good attitude. One way you can do that is by learning about Jesus and about His attitude toward life. When you do, you'll learn that it's always better to think good thoughts, and it's always better to do good things. Always!

God's Amazing Animals: That's an Old Lobster!

Lobsters can live to be 100 years old or older, if fishermen leave them alone.

OBEYING GOD

But be doers of the word and not hearers only.

James 1:22 HCSB

How can you show God how much you love Him? By obeying His commandments, that's how! When you follow God's rules, you show Him that you have real respect for Him and for His Son.

Sometimes, you will be tempted to disobey God, but don't do it. And sometimes you'll be tempted to disobey your parents or your teachers . . . but don't do that, either.

When your parent steps away or a teacher looks away, it's up to you to control yourself. And of this you can be sure: If you really want to control yourself, you can do it!

Happiness is obedience, and obedience is happiness.

C. H. Spurgeon

Pet Facts: Clean Cats!

Cats can spend up to 30% of their waking hours grooming themselves. No wonder they stay clean!

WHEN YOU ARE HURTING

But I will call on God, and the Lord will rescue me. Morning, noon, and night I plead aloud in my distress, and the Lord hears my voice.

Psalm 55:16-17 NLT

Sometimes people can be rude . . . very rude. When other people are unkind to you (or to your friends), you may be tempted to strike back, either verbally or in some other way. Don't do it! Instead, remember that God corrects other people's behaviors in His own way, and He doesn't need your help (even if you think that He does).

As long as you live here on earth, you will face countless opportunities to lose your temper when other folks behave badly. But God has a better plan: He wants you to forgive people and move on. Remember that God has already forgiven you, so it's only right that you should be willing to forgive others.

So, when other people behave cruelly, foolishly, or impulsively—as they will from time to time—don't be hotheaded. Instead, speak up for yourself as politely as you can, and walk away. Then, forgive everybody as quickly as you can, and leave the rest up to God.

Pet Facts: That's a Whole Lot of Dog Food

Great Danes can eat up to eight and a half pounds of food a day.

DON'T GIVE UP!

Thanks be to God! He gives us the victory through our Lord Jesus Christ. Therefore, my dear brothers, stand firm. Let nothing move you. Always give yourselves fully to the work of the Lord, because you know that your labor in the Lord is not in vain.

1 Corinthians 15:57-58 NIV

Are you a girl who doesn't give up easily, or are you quick to bail out when the going gets tough? If you've developed the unfortunate habit of giving up at the first sign of trouble, it's probably time for you to have a heart-to-heart talk with that person you see every time you look in the mirror.

A well-lived life is like a marathon, not a sprint—it calls for preparation, determination, and lots of perseverance. As an example of perfect perseverance, you need look no further than Jesus Christ.

Jesus finished what He began. Despite His suffering and despite the shame of the cross, Jesus was steadfast in His faithfulness to God. You, too, should remain faithful, especially when times are tough.

Are you facing a difficult situation? If so, remember this: whatever your problem, God can handle it. Your job is to keep persevering until He does.

God's Amazing Animals: If You Don't Like Snakes . . .

Antarctica is the only continent without reptiles or snakes.

LEARNING TO CONTROL YOURSELF

But endurance must do its complete work, so that you may be mature and complete, lacking nothing.

James 1:4 HCSB

In the game of life, it's good to be able to control yourself. But if you're having trouble learning how to control your actions or your emotions, you're not alone! Most people have problems with self-control from time to time, so don't be discouraged. Just remember that self-control, like any other skill, requires practice and lots of it. So if you're a little discouraged, don't give up. Just keep working on improving your self-control until you get better at it . . . and if you keep trying, you can be sure that sooner or later, you will get better at it.

Don't give up. Moses was once a basket case!

Anonymous

Pet Facts: Indoor Cats Live Longer

The average lifespan of an outdoor-only cat is about 4 to 6 years. But, an indoor-only cat can live up to 16 years, or much longer.

BE RESPECTFUL

Show respect for all people. Love the brothers and sisters of God's family.

1 Peter 2:17 ICB

Are you polite and respectful to your parents, to your teachers, to your classmates, and to your friends? And do you do your best to treat everybody you meet with the respect they deserve? Hopefully so because that's precisely what your Father in heaven wants you to do.

Respect for others is habit-forming: the more we do it, the easier it becomes. So start practicing right now. Say lots of kind words and do lots of kind things, because when it comes to kindness and respect, practice makes perfect.

God's Amazing Animals:
Faster Chirps Mean Higher Temperatures

If you know how to do it, you can tell the temperature by the speed of a cricket's chirp. The higher the temperature the faster the chirps. When the temperature is 52°F, a cricket chirps about 60 times a minute.

MATERIAL AND SPIRITUAL POSSESSIONS

And how do you benefit if you gain the whole world but lose your own soul in the process? Is anything worth more than your soul?

Mark 8:36-37 NLT

Earthly riches are temporary: here today and soon gone forever. Spiritual riches, on the other hand, are permanent: ours today, ours tomorrow, ours throughout eternity. Yet all too often, we focus our thoughts and energies on the accumulation of earthly treasures, leaving precious little time to accumulate the only treasures that really matter: the spiritual kind.

Our material possessions have the potential to do great good or terrible harm, depending upon how we choose to use them. As believers, our instructions are clear: we must use our possessions in accordance with God's commandments, and we must be faithful stewards of the gifts He has seen fit to bestow upon us.

Today, let us honor God by placing no other gods before Him. God comes first; everything else comes next—and "everything else" most certainly includes all of our earthly possessions.

God's Amazing Animals: Waterproof Outer Wear

Ducks produce oils that make their feathers waterproof.

A ROYAL LAW

This royal law is found in the Scriptures: "Love your neighbor as yourself." If you obey this law, then you are doing right.

James 2:8 ICB

James was the brother of Jesus and a leader of the early Christian church. In a letter that is now a part of the New Testament, James reminded his friends of a "royal law." That law is the Golden Rule.

When we treat others in the same way that we wish to be treated, we are doing the right thing. James knew it and so, of course, did his brother Jesus. Now we should learn the same lesson: it's nice to be nice; it's good to be good; and it's great to be kind.

It doesn't take monumental feats to make the world a better place. It can be as simple as letting someone go ahead of you in a grocery line.

Barbara Johnson

God's Amazing Animals: They're Not Really Dogs

Prairie dogs are rodents, not dogs. However they are called dogs because their warning call sounds like a dog bark.

HONESTY NOW

The honest person will live safely, but the one who is dishonest will be caught.

Proverbs 10:9 ICB

Nobody can tell the truth for you. You're the one who decides what you are going to say. You're the one who decides whether your words will be truthful . . . or not.

If you find yourself tempted to break the truth—or even to bend it—remember that honesty is God's policy . . . and it must also be yours. Simply put, if you really want to walk with God—and if you really want to guard your heart against the dangers of sin—you must protect your integrity very carefully today, tomorrow, and every day after that.

Those who tell white lies soon become color blind.

Anonymous

God's Amazing Animals: Lions Live Longer in Zoos!

In the wild, lions live for an average of 12 years, and sometimes they can live longer than that. But, lions can live up to 25 years in captivity.

FINDING (AND TRUSTING) MENTORS

A wise man will listen and increase his learning, and a discerning man will obtain guidance.

Proverbs 1:5 HCSB

D o you want to become a wise young woman? Then you must acknowledge that you are not wise enough on your own. When you face an important decision, you must first study God's Word, and you should also seek the counsel of trusted friends and mentors.

When we arrive at the inevitable crossroads of life, God inevitably sends righteous men and women to guide us if we let them. If we are willing to listen and to learn, then we, too, will become wise. And God will bless our endeavors.

Do you want to be wise? Choose wise friends.

Charles Swindoll

God's Amazing Animals: Big, Big Lobsters

There are records of full-grown lobsters weighing over 40 pounds!

WHEN THINGS GO WRONG

But as for you, be strong; don't be discouraged, for your work has a reward.

2 Chronicles 15:7 HCSB

Sometimes you win and sometimes you don't, so some days are more wonderful than other days. Sometimes, everything seems to go right, and on other days, many things seem to go wrong. But here's something to remember: even when you're disappointed with the way things turn out, God is near . . . and He loves you very much!

If you're disappointed, worried, sad, or afraid, you can talk to your friends, to your parents, and to God. And you will certainly feel better when you do!

The difference between winning and losing is how we choose to react to disappointment.

Barbara Johnson

God's Amazing Animals: Pigs Are Very Smart!

Most experts believe that pigs are smarter than dogs! In fact, only magpies, chimpanzees, dolphins, whales, and elephants are known to be smarter than pigs.

DEMONSTRATING YOUR FAITH

So brothers and sisters, be careful that none of you has an evil, unbelieving heart that will turn you away from the living God. But encourage each other every day while it is "today." Help each other so none of you will become hardened because sin has tricked you.

Hebrews 3:13 NCV

Let's face facts: those of us who are Christians should be willing to talk about the things that Christ has done for us. Our personal stories are vitally important, but sometimes, because of shyness or insecurities, we're afraid to share our experiences. And that's unfortunate.

We live in a world that desperately needs the healing message of Christ Jesus. Every believer, each in his or her own way, bears responsibility for sharing the Good News of our Savior. And it is important to remember that we bear testimony through both words and actions.

If you seek to be a radical follower of Christ, then it's time for you to share your testimony with others. So today, preach the Gospel through your words and your deeds…but not necessarily in that order.

Pet Facts: What Color Are Your Kitten's Eyes?

Believe it or not, all kittens are born with blue eyes.

KINDNESS STARTS WITH YOU

And be kind and compassionate to one another, forgiving one another, just as God also forgave you in Christ.

Ephesians 4:32 HCSB

If you're waiting for other people to be nice to you before you're nice to them, you've got it backwards. Kindness starts with you! You see, you can never control what other people will say or do, but you can control your own behavior.

The Bible tells us that we should never stop doing good deeds as long as we live. Kindness is God's way, and it should be our way, too.

So today, make sure to put a smile on your face and keep a steady stream of encouraging words on your lips. By blessing others, you will also bless yourself, and when you do, the Creator smiles.

Kind words have echoes that last a lifetime and beyond.

Anonymous

Pet Facts: Dogs Smell Well

Dogs have an amazing sense of smell. Some dogs can tell the difference between different odors that are hundreds of times fainter than odors that humans can smell!

EXPECTING THE IMPOSSIBLE

Is anything impossible for the Lord?

Genesis 18:14 HCSB

Do you believe that God is at work in the world? And do you also believe that nothing is impossible for Him? If so, then you also believe that God is perfectly capable of doing things that you, as a mere human being with limited vision and limited understanding, would deem to be utterly impossible. And that's precisely what God does.

Since He created our universe out of nothingness, God has made a habit of doing miraculous things. And He still works miracles today. Expect Him to work miracles in your own life, and then be watchful. With God, absolutely nothing is impossible, including an amazing assortment of miracles that He stands ready, willing, and able to perform for you and yours.

God's Amazing Animals: Better Than Your Average Dog House

Prairie dogs' burrows are quite large with many entrances and many rooms. In fact, a typical burrow even has separate rooms used as bathrooms, kids' rooms, and bedrooms!

THE JOYS OF A CLEAR CONSCIENCE

Let us come near to God with a sincere heart and a sure faith, because we have been made free from a guilty conscience, and our bodies have been washed with pure water.

Hebrews 10:22 NCV

If we fail to play by God's rules, that little voice inside our heads starts sending out warning signals. And few things in life torment us more than a guilty conscience. On the other hand, few things in life provide more contentment than the knowledge that we are obeying God's commandments.

A clear conscience is one of the rewards we earn when we obey God's Word and follow His will. When we follow God's will and accept His gift of salvation, our earthly rewards are never-ceasing, and our heavenly rewards are everlasting.

Arm yourself with the Word of God, and your conscience will sound off loud and clear when you're headed in the wrong direction.

Charles Stanley

God's Amazing Animals: What Do You Call a Duck?

Boy ducks are called "drakes." Girl ducks are called "hens." And, baby ducks are called "ducklings."

DIRECTING YOUR THOUGHTS!

Set your minds on what is above, not on what is on the earth.

Colossians 3:2 HCSB

D o you direct your thoughts toward things that are honorable, true, and uplifting? The Bible says that you should. Do you lift your hopes and your prayers to God many times each day? The Bible says that you should. Do you turn away from bad thoughts and bad people? The Bible says that you should.

The Bible instructs you to guard your thoughts against things that are hurtful or wrong. And when you turn away from the bad and turn instead toward God and His Son Jesus, you will be protected and you will be blessed.

Surrender your mind to the Lord at the beginning of each day.

Warren Wiersbe

God's Amazing Animals:
Penguins Are Good At Holding Their Breath

Emperor penguins can stay underwater for around 20 minutes without taking a breath of air!

YOU CAN'T PLEASE EVERYBODY

My son, if sinners entice you, don't be persuaded.

Proverbs 1:10 HCSB

Are you one of those people who tries to please everybody in sight? If so, you'd better watch out! After all, if you worry too much about pleasing your friends, you may not worry enough about pleasing God.

Whom will you try to please today: your God or your pals? The answer to that question should be simple. Your first job is to obey God's rules . . . and that means obeying your parents, too!

So don't worry too much about pleasing your friends or neighbors. Try, instead, to please your Heavenly Father and your parents. No exceptions.

True friends will always lift you higher and challenge you to walk in a manner pleasing to our Lord.

Lisa Bevere

God's Amazing Animals: Pigs Don't Perspire

Pigs have no sweat glands and, therefore, do not sweat. That's why they like to roll around in the mud: it cools them off.

DABBLERS BEWARE

I do not consider myself yet to have taken hold of it. But one thing I do: Forgetting what is behind and straining toward what is ahead, I press on toward the goal to win the prize for which God has called me heavenward in Christ Jesus.

Philippians 3:13-14 NIV

Are you fired up with enthusiasm for Jesus? God has given you the gift of eternal life through His Son. In response to God's priceless gift, you are instructed to focus your thoughts, your prayers, and your energies upon God and His only begotten Son. To do so, you must resist the subtle yet powerful temptation to become a "spiritual dabbler."

A person who dabbles in the Christian faith is unwilling to place God in His rightful place: above all other things. Resist that temptation; make God the cornerstone and the touchstone of your life. When you do, He will give you all the strength and wisdom you need to live victoriously for Him.

Pet Facts: Fast, Fast, and Very Fast Dogs

Most dogs are able to run fast. In fact, they can reach speeds of fifteen miles an hour, or more! So don't try to outrun a dog.

HOW OFTEN DO YOU ASK?

Keep asking, and it will be given to you. Keep searching, and you will find. Keep knocking, and the door will be opened to you. For everyone who asks receives, and the one who searches finds, and to the one who knocks, the door will be opened.

Matthew 7:7-8 HCSB

How often do you ask for God's help? Occasionally? Once in awhile? Whenever you experience a crisis? Hopefully not. Hopefully, you have developed the habit of asking for God's assistance early and often. And hopefully, you have learned to seek His guidance in every aspect of your life.

God has promised that when you ask for His help, He will not withhold it. So ask. Ask Him to meet the needs of your day. Ask Him for wisdom. Ask Him to lead you, to protect you, and to correct you. And trust the answers He gives.

God stands at the door and waits. When you knock on His door, He answers. Your task, of course, is to seek His guidance prayerfully, confidently, and often.

God's Amazing Animals: Paddling Along Through Life

Ducks are excellent swimmers because of their webbed feet.

IN SEARCH OF PEACE

Peace I leave with you. My peace I give to you. I do not give to you as the world gives. Your heart must not be troubled or fearful.

John 14:27 HCSB

The beautiful words of John 14:27 promise that Jesus offers us peace, not as the world gives, but as He alone gives. We, as believers, can accept His peace or ignore it.

When we accept the peace of Jesus Christ into our hearts, our lives are transformed. And then, because we possess the gift of peace, we can share that gift with fellow Christians, family members, and friends. If, on the other hand, we choose to ignore the gift of peace—for whatever reason—we simply cannot share what we do not possess.

Today, as a gift to yourself, to your family, and to your friends, claim the inner peace that is your spiritual birthright: the peace of Jesus Christ. It is offered freely; it has been paid for in full; it is yours for the asking. So ask. And then share.

Pet Facts: You Can Know a Cat by Its Nose

The nose pad of every cat has unique tiny ridges that are almost like human fingerprints.

MOUNTAIN-MOVING FAITH

For I assure you: If you have faith the size of a mustard seed, you will tell this mountain, "Move from here to there," and it will move. Nothing will be impossible for you.

Matthew 17:20 HCSB

Have you ever felt your faith in God slipping away? If so, you are not alone. Every life—including yours—is a series of successes and failures, celebrations and disappointments, joys and sorrows. But even when we feel very distant from God, God is never distant from us.

Jesus taught His disciples that if they had faith, they could move mountains. You can too. When you place your faith, your trust, indeed your life in the hands of Christ Jesus, you'll be amazed at the marvelous things He can do with you and through you. So strengthen your faith through praise, through worship, through Bible study, and through prayer. And trust God's plans. With Him, all things are possible, and He stands ready to open a world of possibilities to you if you have faith.

God's Amazing Animals: Early Warning System

Prairie dogs warn each other about approaching danger by letting out special warning barks!

HOW DO THEY KNOW?

Even a child is known by his behavior. His actions show if he is innocent and good.

Proverbs 20:11 ICB

As you play the game of life, people are watching. So how do other people know that you're a Christian? Well, you can tell them, of course. And make no mistake about it: talking about your faith in God is a very good thing to do. But simply telling people about Jesus isn't enough. You must also be willing to show people how a real Christian (like you) should behave. Does that sound like a big responsibility? It is . . . but you can do it! And you should do it because actions always speak louder than words. Always!

As we live moment by moment under the control of the Spirit, His character, which is the character of Jesus, becomes evident to those around us.

Anne Graham Lotz

God's Amazing Animals: What Does an Elephant Do with Its Trunk?

Elephants use their trunks to determine the size, shape, and temperature of the things they pick up. They also use their trunks to pick up food and suck up water, which they then pour into their mouths.

A THANKFUL HEART

Enter his gates with thanksgiving; go into his courts with praise. Give thanks to him and bless his name. For the Lord is good. His unfailing love continues forever, and his faithfulness continues to each generation.

Psalm 100:4-5 NLT

If you're like most people on the planet, you're very busy. But, no matter how busy you are, you should never be too busy to thank God for His gifts. Your task, as a follower of the living Christ, is to praise God many times each day. Then, with gratitude in your heart, you can face your daily duties with the perspective and power that only He can provide.

When you slow down and express your gratitude to your Heavenly Father, you enrich your own life and the lives of those around you. That's why thanksgiving should become a habit, a regular part of your daily routine. Yes, God has blessed you beyond measure, and you owe Him everything, including your eternal praise.

God's Amazing Animals:
Before You Get Sprayed, You'll Get Warned

A skunk usually gives a warning before spraying. It turns its back to the target, hisses, and stamps its feet.

THE OPTIMISTIC CHRISTIAN

Make me hear joy and gladness.

Psalm 51:8 NKJV

As a Christian, you have every reason to be optimistic about life. As John Calvin observed, "There is not one blade of grass, there is no color in this world that is not intended to make us rejoice." But, sometimes, rejoicing may be the last thing on your mind. Sometimes, you may fall prey to worry, frustration, anxiety, or sheer exhaustion. What's needed is plenty of rest, a large dose of perspective, and God's healing touch, but not necessarily in that order.

A. W. Tozer writes, "Attitude is all-important. Let the soul take a quiet attitude of faith and love toward God, and from there on, the responsibility is God's. He will make good on His commitments." These words remind us that even when the challenges of the day seem daunting, God remains steadfast. And, so must we.

God's Amazing Animals: That's a Lot of Ants

In California, an amazing collection of Argentine ants has built what scientists believe may be the biggest ant colony in the world, stretching more than 600 miles from San Diego to San Francisco.

FINDING TIME FOR GOD

I am always praising you; all day long I honor you.

Psalm 71:8 NCV

Each new day is a gift from God, and if we are wise, we spend a few quiet moments each morning thanking the Giver. Daily life is a tapestry of habits, and no habit is more important to our spiritual health than the discipline of daily prayer and devotion to the Creator. When we begin each day with heads bowed and hearts lifted, we remind ourselves of God's love, His protection, and His commandments. And if we are wise, we take time throughout the day to align our priorities with the teachings and commandments that God has given us through His Holy Word.

Are you thankful for God's blessings? Then give Him a gift that demonstrates your gratitude: the gift of time.

Jesus challenges you and me to keep our focus daily on the cross of His will if we want to be His disciples.

Anne Graham Lotz

Pet Facts: A Dog's Life

The average life span for a typical dog is about 10 to 14 years.

FAITH WITHOUT WORKS

In the same way faith, if it doesn't have works, is dead by itself.

James 2:17 HCSB

The central message of James' letter is the need for believers to act upon their beliefs. James' instruction is clear: "faith without works is dead." We are saved by our faith in Christ, but salvation does not signal the end of our earthly responsibilities; it marks the true beginning of our work for the Lord.

If your faith in God is strong, you will find yourself drawn toward God's work. You will serve Him, not just with words or prayers, but also with deeds. Because of your faith, you will feel compelled to do God's work—to do it gladly, faithfully, joyfully, and consistently.

Today, redouble your efforts to do God's bidding here on earth. Never have the needs—or the opportunities—been greater.

God's Amazing Animals: How Big Are Prairie Dogs?

Prairie dogs are usually about 15 inches long, and they usually weigh between 2 and 4 pounds.

IT'S A GOOD FEELING TO OBEY AND FORGIVE

For this is what love for God is: to keep His commands. Now His commands are not a burden, because whatever has been born of God conquers the world. This is the victory that has conquered the world: our faith.

1 John 5:3-4 HCSB

We know that it's right to forgive other people and wrong to stay angry with them. But sometimes, it's so much easier to do the wrong thing than it is to do the right thing, especially when we're tired or frustrated.

When you do the right thing by forgiving other people, you'll feel good because you'll know that you're obeying God. And that's a very good feeling indeed.

So today and every day, make this promise to yourself and keep it: play by the rules—God's rules. You'll always be glad you did.

God's Amazing Animals: How Frogs See the World

Frogs can see straight ahead, sideways, and upwards, all at the same time. And, frogs don't close their eyes when they sleep.

SHARING LOVE AND KINDNESS

Talk and act like a person expecting to be judged by the Rule that sets us free. For if you refuse to act kindly, you can hardly expect to be treated kindly. Kind mercy wins over harsh judgment every time.

James 2:12-13 MSG

Where does kindness start? It starts in our hearts and works its way out from there. Jesus taught us that a pure heart is a wonderful blessing. It's up to each of us to fill our hearts with love for God, love for Jesus, and love for all people. When we do, we are blessed.

Do you want to be the best person you can be? Then invite the love of Christ into your heart and share His love with your family, your friends, and the world. And remember that lasting love always comes from a pure heart like yours!

Pet Facts: Hamster Marathons

In the cool of the evening, wild hamsters search for food. Amazingly, they can travel up to 8 miles in a single night.

FOLLOW JESUS

"Follow Me," Jesus told them, "and I will make you into fishers of men!" Immediately they left their nets and followed Him.

Mark 1:17-18 HCSB

Here's a very important question that only you can answer: Who will you walk with today? Do yourself a favor—walk with Jesus!

God's Word promises that when you follow in Christ's footsteps, you will learn how to behave yourself, and you'll learn how to live a good life. Jesus wants you to be a "new creation" through Him. And that's exactly what you should want for yourself, too. So talk with Jesus (through prayer) and walk with Him (by obeying His rules) today and forever.

We must go out and live among them, manifesting the gentle, loving spirit of our Lord. We need to make friends before we can hope to make converts.

Lottie Moon

God's Amazing Animals: Why Do Skunks Spray?

Skunks don't spray to be mean. They only spray in self-defense.

THE BREAD OF LIFE

Then Jesus said, "I am the bread that gives life. Whoever comes to me will never be hungry, and whoever believes in me will never be thirsty."

John 6:35 NCV

He was the Son of God, but He wore a crown of thorns. He was the Savior of mankind, yet He was put to death on a roughhewn cross made of wood. He offered His healing touch to an unsaved world, and yet the same hands that had healed the sick and raised the dead were pierced with nails.

Jesus Christ, the Son of God, was born into humble circumstances. He walked this earth, not as a ruler of men, but as the Savior of mankind. His crucifixion, a torturous punishment that was intended to end His life and His reign, instead became the pivotal event in the history of all humanity.

Jesus is the bread of life. Accept His grace. Share His love. And follow His footsteps.

God's Amazing Animals: That's a Big Baby!

A baby elephant can weigh over 250 pounds when it's born.

THE POWER OF PRAYER

Therefore I say to you, whatever things you ask when you pray, believe that you receive them, and you will have them.

Mark 11:24 NKJV

In case you've been wondering, wonder no more—God does answer your prayers. What God does not do is this: He does not always answer your prayers as soon as you might like, and He does not always answer your prayers by saying "Yes."

God isn't an order-taker, and He's not some sort of cosmic vending machine. Sometimes—even when we want something very badly—our loving Heavenly Father responds to our requests by saying "No," and we must accept His answer, even if we don't understand it.

God answers prayers not only according to our wishes but also according to His master plan. We cannot know that plan, but we can know the Planner . . . and we must trust His wisdom, His righteousness, and His love. Of this you can be sure: God is listening, and He wants to hear from you now.

Pet Facts: Nighttime Is the Right Time for Cats to See Better Than People

Cats see six times better in the dark than humans do.

WHEN IN DOUBT . . .

Don't depend on your own wisdom. Respect the Lord and refuse to do wrong.

Proverbs 3:7 NCV

If you're like most young people, you're busy . . . very busy. And sometimes, because so much is expected of you, you may lose perspective. Your life may seem to be spinning out of control, and the pressures of everyday living seem overwhelming. What's needed is a fresh perspective, a restored sense of balance . . . and God's wisdom.

Would you really like to become wise? If so, learning about wisdom isn't enough. You must also behave wisely. Wisdom is as wisdom does. Wisdom is determined, not by words, but by deeds.

Do you wish to walk among the wise? If so, you must walk wisely. There is simply no other way.

Pet Facts: Need Two Coats?

Some dogs have not one but two coats. The outer coat is usually longer while the undercoat is shorter and fluffier. These two coats protect the dog against rain and snow. Puppies are born helpless. They cannot see, and they cannot stand up. So how do puppies spend their days? Sleeping! They sleep almost all day long.

LOVING PEOPLE WHO ARE HARD TO LOVE

You have heard that it was said, You shall love your neighbor and hate your enemy. But I tell you, love your enemies, and pray for those who persecute you, so that you may be sons of your Father in heaven.

Matthew 5:43-45 HCSB

In the game of life, not everybody plays by the rules. Sometimes people can be dishonest, or rude, or both. As long as you live here on earth, you will face countless opportunities to lose your temper when other folks behave badly. But God has a better plan: He wants you to forgive people and move on. Remember that God has already forgiven you, so it's only right that you should be willing to forgive others.

So here's some good advice: Forgive everybody as quickly as you can, and leave the rest up to God.

You can be sure you are abiding in Christ if you are able to have a Christlike love toward the people that irritate you the most.

Vonette Bright

God's Amazing Animals: What Do Prairie Dogs Eat?

Prairie dogs eat roots, grass, and other plants.

WHEN TIMES ARE TOUGH

I have told you these things so that in Me you may have peace. In the world you have suffering. But take courage! I have conquered the world.

John 16:33 HCSB

The Bible promises this: tough times are temporary but God's love is not—God's love lasts forever. So what does that mean to you? Just this: From time to time, everybody faces tough times, and so will you. And when tough times arrive, God will always stand ready to protect you and heal you.

Psalm 147 promises, "He heals the brokenhearted" (v. 3, NIV), but Psalm 147 doesn't say that He heals them instantly. Usually, it takes time (and maybe even a little help from you) for God to fix things. So if you're facing tough times, face them with God by your side. If you find yourself in any kind of trouble, pray about it and ask God for help. And be patient. God will work things out, just as He has promised, but He will do it in His own way and in His own time.

Pet Facts: A Very Short Tale About a Cat's Tail

How do cats use their tails? Tails help cats keep their balance. The end.

PRAISING GOD'S GLORIOUS CREATION

The heavens declare the glory of God, and the sky proclaims the work of His hands.

Psalm 19:1 HCSB

Each morning, the sun rises upon a glorious world that is a physical demonstration of God's infinite power and His infinite love. And yet we're sometimes too busy to notice.

We live in a society filled with more distractions than we can possibly count and more obligations than we can possibly meet. Is it any wonder, then, that we often overlook God's handiwork as we rush from place to place, giving scarcely a single thought to the beauty that surrounds us?

Today, take time to really observe the world around you. Take time to offer a pray of thanks for the sky above and the beauty that lies beneath it. And take time to ponder the miracle of God's creation. The time you spend celebrating God's wonderful world is always time well spent.

Pet Facts: Building Up Your Dog's Self-image

Just like people, dogs can develop a poor self-image if they're not treated well. You can increase your dog's self-esteem with praise, affection, petting, and rewards.

GOD'S TIMETABLE

There is an occasion for everything, and a time for every activity under heaven.

Ecclesiastes 3:1 HCSB

As busy people living in a fast-paced world, many of us find that waiting quietly for God is difficult. Why? Because we are imperfect human beings seeking to live according to our own timetables, not God's. In our better moments, we realize that patience is not only a virtue, but it is also a commandment from the Creator.

God instructs us to be patient in all things. We must be patient with our families, with our friends, and with our acquaintances. We must also be patient with our Heavenly Father as He unfolds His plan for our lives. And that's as it should be. After all, think how patient God has been with us.

Living by faith requires patience, for the one who lives by faith becomes dependent upon God.

Kay Arthur

God's Amazing Animals: Why Halloween Isn't a Cat's Favorite Holiday

Don't ever feed your cat candy. Some candies can be poisonous, and besides, cats can't even taste sweets.

IT'S GOOD FOR YOU

So I recommend having fun, because there is nothing better for people to do in this world than to eat, drink, and enjoy life. That way they will experience some happiness along with all the hard work God gives them.

Ecclesiastes 8:15 NLT

Sometimes, we may feel guilty about having fun when some people around the world are not having any fun at all. But God doesn't want us to spend our lives moping around with frowns on our faces. Far from it! God tells us that a happy heart is a very good thing to have.

So if you're afraid to laugh out loud, don't be. Remember that God wouldn't have given you the gift of laughter if He hadn't intended for you to use it. And remember: if you're laughing, that does not mean that you're unconcerned about people who may be hurting. It simply means that you've taken a little time to have fun, and that's good because God wants you to have a cheerful heart.

Proverbs 17:22 says that laughter is good medicine. Do yourself a favor and take that medicine whenever you can.

God's Amazing Animals: Fast-Moving Herds

An elephant herd can travel 50 miles in a day.

THIS IS THE DAY

This is the day the Lord has made; let us rejoice and be glad in it.

Psalm 118:24 HCSB

Are you basically a thankful person? Do you appreciate the stuff you've got and the life that you're privileged to live? You most certainly should be thankful. After all, when you stop to think about it, God has given you more blessings than you can count. So the question of the day is this: will you slow down long enough to thank your Heavenly Father . . . or not?

Sometimes, life here on earth can be complicated, demanding, and frustrating. When the demands of life leave you rushing from place to place with scarcely a moment to spare, you may fail to pause and thank your Creator for the countless blessings He has given you. Failing to thank God is understandable . . . but it's wrong.

God's Word makes it clear: a wise heart is a thankful heart. Period. Your Heavenly Father has blessed you beyond measure, and you owe Him everything, including your thanks. God is always listening—are you willing to say thanks? It's up to you, and the next move is yours.

God's Amazing Animals: For the Birds!

Many birds eat twice their weight a day.

THE POWER OF OUR THOUGHTS

People's thoughts can be like a deep well, but someone with understanding can find the wisdom there.

Proverbs 20:5 NCV

O ur thoughts have the power to shape our lives—for better or for worse. Thoughts have the power to lift our spirits, to improve our circumstances, and to strengthen our relationship with the Creator. But, our thoughts also have the power to cause us great harm if we focus too intently upon those things that distance us from God.

Today, make your thoughts an offering to God. Seek—by the things you think and the actions you take—to honor Him and serve Him. He deserves no less. And neither, for that matter, do you.

The things we think are the things that feed our souls. If we think on pure and lovely things, we shall grow pure and lovely like them; and the converse is equally true.

Hannah Whitall Smith

God's Amazing Animals: A Mighty Big Tongue

A blue whale's tongue is big. In fact, most elephants weigh less than the tongue of a fully-grown blue whale.

GOD MAKES ALL THINGS POSSIBLE

You are the God who works wonders; You revealed Your strength among the peoples.

Psalm 77:14 HCSB

Sometimes, because we are imperfect human beings with limited understanding and limited faith, we place limitations on God. But, God's power has no limitations. God will work miracles in our lives if we trust Him with everything we have and everything we are. When we do, we experience the miraculous results of His endless love and His awesome power.

Do you lack the faith that God can work miracles in your own life? If so, it's time to reconsider. Are you a "Negative Nellie"? If so, you are attempting to place limitations on a God who has none. Instead, you must trust in God and trust in His power. Then, you must wait patiently . . . because something miraculous is just about to happen.

Pet Facts: Strong Ears, in More Ways Than One

It's pretty obvious that dogs have good hearing. But, what's not so obvious is that dogs have more muscles in their ears! In fact, dogs have twice as many muscles for moving their ears as humans do.

WHEN YOU DON'T KNOW WHAT TO SAY

Watch the way you talk. Let nothing foul or dirty come out of your mouth. Say only what helps, each word a gift.

Ephesians 4:29 MSG

Sometimes, it's hard to know exactly what to say. And sometimes, it can be very tempting to say something that isn't true—or something that isn't polite. But when you say things you shouldn't say, you'll regret it later.

So make this promise to yourself, and keep it—promise to think about the things you say before you say them. And whatever you do, always tell the truth. When you do these things, you'll be doing yourself a big favor, and you'll be obeying the Word of God.

When you talk, choose the very same words that you would use if Jesus were looking over your shoulder. Because He is.

Marie T. Freeman

Pet Facts: How Long Do Hamsters Live?

A hamster's normal lifespan is about 2 or 3 years, but they sometimes live to be 4 years old.

QUIET TIME

Rest in God alone, my soul, for my hope comes from Him.

Psalm 62:5 HCSB

The world can be a noisy place, a place filled to the brim with distractions, interruptions, and frustrations. And if you're not careful, the struggles and stresses of everyday living can rob you of the peace that should rightfully be yours because of your personal relationship with Christ.

So take time each day to have a quiet heart-to-heart talk with your Savior. When you do, those moments of silence will enable you to participate more fully in the only source of peace that endures: God's peace.

When an honest soul can get still before the living Christ, we can still hear Him say simply and clearly, "Love the Lord your God with all your heart and with all your soul and with all your mind . . . and love one another as I have loved you."

Gloria Gaither

God's Amazing Animals: A Dog Food Fact

Americans spend more money on dog food each year than they do on baby food.

INCLUDE GOD IN YOUR PLANS

Depend on the Lord in whatever you do, and your plans will succeed.

Proverbs 16:3 NCV

Would you like a formula for successful living that never fails? Here it is: Include God in every aspect of your life's journey, including the plans that you make and the steps that you take. But beware: as you make plans for the days and weeks ahead, you may become sidetracked by the demands of everyday living.

If you allow the world to establish your priorities, you will eventually become discouraged, or disappointed, or both. But if you genuinely seek God's will for every important decision that you make, your loving Heavenly Father will guide your steps and enrich your life. So as you plan your day, remember that every good plan should start with God, including yours.

God's Amazing Animals: A Very Strong Beetle

The rhinoceros beetle can support up to 850 times its own weight on its back. That would be the equivalent of a man carrying over 50 cars around on his back.

KEEPING POSSESSIONS IN PERSPECTIVE

No one can serve two masters. The person will hate one master and love the other, or will follow one master and refuse to follow the other. You cannot serve both God and worldly riches.

Matthew 6:24 NCV

"So much stuff to shop for, and so little time." These words seem to describe the priorities of our world. Hopefully, you're not building your life around your next visit to the local mall—but you can be sure that many people are!

Our society is in love with money and the things that money can buy. God is not. God cares about people, not possessions, and so must we. We must, to the best of our abilities, love our neighbors as ourselves, and we must, to the best of our abilities, resist the mighty temptation to place possessions ahead of people.

Money, in and of itself, is not evil; worshipping money is. So today, as you prioritize matters of importance for you and yours, remember that God is almighty, but the dollar is not.

God's Amazing Animals: Chimps Can Live a Long Time

Chimpanzees can live for 50 years or more! Usually, they live longer in zoos than in the wild.

WITH ALL YOUR HEART AND SOUL

Love the LORD your God with all your heart and with all your soul and with all your strength.

Deuteronomy 6:5 NIV

God's love for you is bigger and stronger than you can imagine. God's love for you is so great that He sent His only Son to this earth to die for your sins and to offer you the priceless gift of eternal life. Now, you must decide whether or not to accept God's gift. Will you ignore it or embrace it? Will you return it or neglect it? Will you accept Christ's love and build a lifelong relationship with Him, or will you turn away from Him and take a different path?

Your decision to allow Christ to reign over your heart is the pivotal decision of your life. It is a decision that you cannot ignore. It is a decision that is yours and yours alone. Accept God's gift now: allow His Son to preside over your heart, your thoughts, and your life, starting this very instant.

God's Amazing Animals: Elks Are Big

The American elk is the second biggest member of the deer family (only the moose is bigger). A big elk can weigh up to 700 pounds.

MIRACLES GREAT AND SMALL

For nothing will be impossible with God.

Luke 1:37 HCSB

God is a miracle worker. Throughout history He has intervened in the course of human events in ways that cannot be explained by science or human rationale. And He's still doing so today.

God's miracles are not limited to special occasions, nor are they witnessed by a select few. God is crafting His wonders all around us: the miracle of the birth of a new baby; the miracle of a world renewing itself with every sunrise; the miracle of lives transformed by God's love and grace. Each day, God's handiwork is evident for all to see and experience.

Today, seize the opportunity to inspect God's hand at work. His miracles come in a variety of shapes and sizes, so keep your eyes and your heart open. Be watchful, and you'll soon be amazed.

God's Amazing Animals: Possums Have Big Families

The opossum gives birth to as many as 15 babies at a time. After birth, opossum babies crawl up into their mother's pouch where they continue to grow until they are a few months old.

A CONTINUAL FEAST?

A cheerful heart has a continual feast.

Proverbs 15:15 HCSB

What is a continual feast? It's a little bit like a non-stop celebration: fun, fun, and more fun! The Bible tells us that a cheerful heart can make life like a continual feast, and that's something worth working for.

Where does cheerfulness begin? It begins inside each of us; it begins in the heart. So today and every day, let's be thankful to God for His blessings, and let's show our thanks by sharing good cheer wherever we go. This old world needs all the cheering up it can get . . . and so do we!

When we bring sunshine into the lives of others, we're warmed by it ourselves. When we spill a little happiness, it splashes on us.

Barbara Johnson

Pet Facts: Long-Distance Hearing

A dog can hear sounds 250 yards away that most people cannot hear beyond 25 yards.

SELF-CONTROL AND PATIENCE

All athletes practice strict self-control. They do it to win a prize that will fade away, but we do it for an eternal prize.

1 Corinthians 9:25 NLT

The Bible tells us time and again that self-control and patience are very good things to have. But for most of us, self-control and patience can also be very hard things to learn.

Are you having trouble being patient? And are you having trouble slowing down long enough to think before you act? If so, remember that self-control takes practice, and lots of it, so keep trying. And if you make a mistake, don't be too upset. After all, if you're going to be a really patient person, you shouldn't just be patient with others; you should also be patient with yourself.

Your thoughts are the determining factor as to whose mold you are conformed to. Control your thoughts and you control the direction of your life.

Charles Stanley

Pet Facts: Cats Are Fast, Especially When They're Scared

A frightened cat can run at speeds of up to 31 mph, slightly faster than a human sprinter.

HOW THEY KNOW THAT WE KNOW

But whoever keeps His word, truly in him the love of God is perfected. This is how we know we are in Him: the one who says he remains in Him should walk just as He walked.

1 John 2:5-6 HCSB

How do others know that we are followers of Christ? By our words and by our actions. And when it comes to proclaiming our faith, the actions we take are far more important than the proclamations we make.

Is your conduct a worthy example for believers and non-believers alike? Is your behavior a testimony to the spiritual abundance that is available to those who allow Christ to reign over their hearts? If so, you are wise: congratulations. But if you're like most of us, then you know that some important aspect of your life could stand improvement. If so, today is the perfect day to make yourself a living, breathing example of the wonderful changes that Christ can make in the lives of those who choose to walk with Him.

God's Amazing Animals: A High-rise Termite Mound

Australian termites have been known to build mounds 20 feet high.

THE COMPANY YOU KEEP

Do not be deceived: "Bad company corrupts good morals."

1 Corinthians 15:33 HCSB

Our world is filled with pressures: some good, some bad. The pressures that we feel to follow God's will and to behave responsibly are positive pressures. God places them on our hearts, and He intends that we act accordingly. But we also face different pressures, ones that are definitely not from God. When we feel pressured to do things—or even to think thoughts—that lead us away from God, we must beware.

Society seeks to mold us into the cookie-cutter images that are the product of the modern media. God seeks to mold us into new beings, new creations through Christ, beings that are most certainly not conformed to this world. If we are to please God, we must resist the pressures that society seeks to impose upon us, and we must conform ourselves, instead, to His will, to His path, and to His Son.

God's Amazing Animals: King-sized Lizards

Komodo dragons are the biggest lizards on earth. Full-grown, they can be 10 feet long and weigh over 300 pounds!

OBEDIENCE IS A CHOICE

Those who obey his commands live in him, and he in them. And this is how we know that he lives in us: We know it by the Spirit he gave us.

1 John 3:24 NIV

You have a choice to make: are you going to be an obedient girl or not? The decision to be obedient is a decision that you must make for yourself.

If you decide to behave yourself you've made a smart choice. If you decide to obey your parents, you've made another smart choice. If you decide to pay attention to your teachers, you've made yet another wise choice. BUT . . . if you decide not to be obedient, you've made a silly choice.

What kind of person will you choose to be? An obedient, well-behaved person . . . or the opposite? Before you answer that question, here's something to think about: obedience pays . . . and disobedience doesn't.

God's Amazing Animals:
Their Feet Are Stronger Than Their Hands

Chimpanzees use both their hands and feet to climb quickly up trees and to swing from branch to branch. Chimps' feet are actually stronger than their hands.

HOLINESS BEFORE HAPPINESS

Blessed are those who hunger and thirst for righteousness, because they will be filled.

Matthew 5:6 HCSB

Because you are an imperfect human being, you are not "perfectly" happy—and that's perfectly okay with God. He is far less concerned with your happiness than He is with your holiness.

God continuously reveals Himself in everyday life, but He does not do so in order to make you contented; He does so in order to lead you to His Son. So don't be overly concerned with your current level of happiness: it will change. Be more concerned with the current state of your relationship with Christ: He does not change. And because your Savior transcends time and space, you can be comforted in the knowledge that in the end, His joy will become your joy . . . for all eternity.

Pet Facts: Dogs Can Tell Time ... Sort Of

Dogs know more about time than you might think. They know when it's time for you to arrive home, when it's time to eat, and when it's time to go to bed. That's why it's helpful if you can get your dog on a regular schedule.

REALLY LIVING MEANS REALLY LOVING

And may the Lord cause you to increase and overflow with love for one another and for everyone, just as we also do for you.

1 Thessalonians 3:12 HCSB

C hrist's words are clear: we are to love God first, and secondly, we are to love others as we love ourselves (Matthew 22:37-40). These two commands are seldom easy, and because we are far from perfect, we often fall short. But God's Holy Word commands us to try.

The Christian path is an exercise in love and forgiveness. If we are to walk in Christ's footsteps, we must forgive those who have done us harm, and we must accept Christ's love by sharing it freely with family, friends, neighbors, and strangers.

A little rain can strengthen a flower stem. A little love can change a life.

Max Lucado

God's Amazing Animals: That's a Big, Old Tortoise!

Giant tortoises of the Galapagos Islands weigh almost 500 pounds and can live for over 150 years.

PRAYERFUL PATIENCE

The Lord is good to those whose hope is in him, to the one who seeks him; it is good to wait quietly for the salvation of the Lord.

Lamentations 3:25-26 NIV

Lamentations 3:25-26 reminds us that it is good to wait quietly for God. But for most of us, waiting patiently for Him is difficult. Why? Because we are fallible human beings with a long list of earthly desires and a definite timetable for obtaining them.

The next time you find yourself impatiently waiting for God to reveal Himself, remember that the world unfolds according to His timetable, not ours. Sometimes, we must wait, and when we do, we should do so quietly and patiently. And, as we consider God's love for us and the perfection of His plans, we can be comforted in the certain knowledge that His timing is perfect, even if our patience is not.

You're in a hurry. God is not. Trust God.

Anonymous

Pet Facts:
The Results from the Pet Popularity Contest Are . . .

Cats win! In 1987, cats overtook dogs as the most popular pet in America.

WHAT YOUR CONSCIENCE SAYS ABOUT FORGIVENESS

Now the goal of our instruction is love from a pure heart, a good conscience, and a sincere faith.

1 Timothy 1:5 HCSB

Your conscience will usually tell you what to do and when to do it. Trust that feeling. Your conscience is usually right.

The world holds few if any rewards for those who remain angrily focused upon the past. Still, the act of forgiveness is difficult for all but the most saintly men and women. Are you mired in the quicksand of bitterness or regret? If so, you are not only disobeying God's Word, you are also wasting your time.

If you listen to your conscience, it won't be as hard for you to forgive people. Why? Because forgiving other people is the right thing to do. And, it's what God wants you to do. And it's what your conscience tells you to do. So what are you waiting for?

God's Amazing Animals: About Beavers

Beavers are rodents. Adult beavers usually weigh between 30 and 60 pounds. They are about 2 to 3 feet long, not including their tails.

ASKING AND ACCEPTING

So I say to you, keep asking, and it will be given to you. Keep searching, and you will find. Keep knocking, and the door will be opened to you.

Luke 11:9 HCSB

God gives the gifts; we, as believers, should accept them—but oftentimes, we don't. Why? Because we fail to trust our Heavenly Father completely, and because we are, at times, surprisingly stubborn. Luke 11 teaches us that God does not withhold spiritual gifts from those who ask. Our obligation, quite simply, is to ask for them.

Are you asking God to move mountains in your life, or are you expecting Him to push over a few molehills? Whatever the size of your challenges, God is big enough to handle them. Ask for His help today, with faith and with fervor, and then watch in amazement as your mountains begin to move.

God's Amazing Animals: That's a Very Big Herd!

One of the largest herds of caribou in the United States is the Porcupine caribou herd that spends most of the time in the Arctic National Wildlife Refuge. This herd has around 123,000 animals; it travels around in an area that's almost 100,000 square miles.

WHEN FRIENDS BEHAVE BADLY

Whoever walks with the wise will become wise; whoever walks with fools will suffer harm.

Proverbs 13:20 NLT

If you're like most people, you have probably been tempted to "go along with the crowd" . . . even when the crowd was misbehaving. But here's something to think about: just because your friends may be misbehaving doesn't mean that you have to misbehave, too.

When people behave badly, they can spoil things in a hurry. So make sure that they don't spoil things for you.

So, if your friends misbehave, don't copy them! Instead, do the right thing. You'll be glad you did . . . and so will God!

It is comfortable to know that we are responsible to God and not to man. It is a small matter to be judged of man's judgement.

Lottie Moon

God's Amazing Animals:
It's an Animal with Eight Very Long Legs!

The world's largest octopus grows from the size of a pea to 150 pounds in just two years. Fully grown, it's 30 feet across.

BUILDING CHARACTER, MOMENT BY MOMENT

May integrity and uprightness protect me, because my hope is in you.

Psalm 25:21 NIV

It has been said that character is what we are when nobody is watching. How true. But, as Bill Hybels correctly observed, "Every secret act of character, conviction, and courage has been observed in living color by our omniscient God." And isn't that a sobering thought?

When we do things that we know aren't right, we try to hide our misdeeds from family members and friends. But even then, God is watching.

If you sincerely wish to walk with God, you must seek, to the best of your ability, to follow His commandments. When you do, your character will take care of itself . . . and you won't need to look over your shoulder to see who, besides God, is watching.

God's Amazing Animals: Busy Builders

Beavers are experts at building dams. Why do they build them? To create safe homes for themselves and their families.

THE TIME TO DO
THE RIGHT THING IS NOW

So don't get tired of doing what is good. Don't get discouraged and give up, for we will reap a harvest of blessing at the appropriate time.

Galatians 6:9 NLT

The old saying is both familiar and true: actions speak louder than words. And as believers, we must beware: our actions should always give credence to the changes that Christ can make in the lives of those who walk with Him.

God calls upon each of us to act in accordance with His will and with respect for His commandments. If we are to be responsible believers, we must realize that it is never enough simply to hear the instructions of God; we must also live by them. And it is never enough to wait idly by while others do God's work here on earth; we, too, must act. Doing God's work is a responsibility that each of us must bear, and when we do, our loving Heavenly Father rewards our efforts with a bountiful harvest.

God's Amazing Animals: Florida's Favorite Big Cat

The panther is Florida's state animal. But, it is estimated that less than 100 panthers still live in the wild.

FINDING THE PURPOSE BENEATH THE PROBLEM

Be joyful because you have hope. Be patient when trouble comes, and pray at all times.

Romans 12:12 NCV

In the game of life, you're bound to encounter a few problems. But hidden beneath every problem is the seed of a solution—God's solution. Your challenge, as a faithful believer, is to trust God's providence and seek His solutions. When you do, you will eventually discover that God does nothing without a very good reason: His reason.

Are you willing to faithfully trust God on good days and bad ones? Hopefully so, because an important part of walking with God is finding His purpose in the midst of your problems.

God's Amazing Animals: About Walruses

Walruses live near the Arctic Circle. They have long tusks and big mustaches. These large marine mammals are found near the Arctic Circle. They are extremely social and snort and bellow loudly at their companions. But don't try to pet one; they're also extremely dangerous!

OBEDIENCE TO GOD

But prove yourselves doers of the word, and not merely hearers.

James 1:22 NASB

God's commandments are not "suggestions," and they are not "helpful hints." They are, instead, immutable laws which, if followed, lead to repentance, salvation, and abundance. But if you choose to disobey the commandments of your Heavenly Father or the teachings of His Son, you will most surely reap a harvest of regret.

The formula for a successful life is surprisingly straightforward: Study God's Word and obey it. Does this sound too simple? Perhaps it is simple, but it is also the only way to reap the marvelous riches that God has in store for you.

Obedience invites Christ to show his incomparable strength in our mortal weakness.

Beth Moore

Pet Facts: Bluey Was a Very Old Dog!

The oldest reliably recorded age of a dog is 29 years and 5 months. The dog was a Queensland heeler named "Bluey."

OUR PROBLEMS = GOD'S OPPORTUNITIES

As for God, his way is perfect. All the LORD's promises prove true. He is a shield for all who look to him for protection.

Psalm 18:30 NLT

Here's a riddle: What is it that is too unimportant to pray about yet too big for God to handle? The answer, of course, is: "nothing." Yet sometimes, when the challenges of the day seem overwhelming, we may spend more time worrying about our troubles than praying about them. And, we may spend more time fretting about our problems than solving them. A far better strategy is to pray as if everything depended entirely upon God and to work as if everything depended entirely upon us.

What we see as problems God sees as opportunities. And if we are to trust Him completely, we must acknowledge that even when our own vision is dreadfully impaired, His vision is perfect. Today and every day, let us trust God by courageously confronting the things that we see as problems and He sees as possibilities.

God's Amazing Animals: Making Honey Is Hard

A bee must visit about 4,000 flowers to make one tablespoon of honey.

NOBODY'S PERFECT

For everything created by God is good, and nothing should be rejected if it is received with thanksgiving.

1 Timothy 4:4 HCSB

Face facts: nobody's perfect . . . not even you! And remember this: it's perfectly okay not to be perfect. In fact, God doesn't expect you to be perfect, and you shouldn't expect yourself to be perfect, either.

Are you one of those people who can't stand to make a mistake? Do you think that you must please everybody all the time? When you make a mess of things, do you become terribly upset? If so, here's some advice: DON'T BE SO HARD ON YOURSELF! Mistakes happen . . . and besides, if you learn something from your mistakes, you'll become a better person.

God is so inconceivably good. He's not looking for perfection. He already saw it in Christ. He's looking for affection.

Beth Moore

God's Amazing Animals: Thirsty?

Camels can go for two months without water.

SCATTERING SEEDS OF KINDNESS

Be devoted to one another in brotherly love. Honor one another above yourselves.

Romans 12:10 NIV

What is a friend? The dictionary defines the word *friend* as "a person who is attached to another by feelings of affection or personal regard." This definition is accurate, as far as it goes, but when we examine the deeper meaning of friendship, so many more descriptors come to mind: trustworthiness, loyalty, helpfulness, kindness, understanding, forgiveness, encouragement, humor, and cheerfulness, to mention but a few.

How wonderful are the joys of friendship. Today, as you consider the many blessings that God has given you, remember to thank Him for the friends He has chosen to place along your path. May you be a blessing to them, and may they richly bless you today, tomorrow, and every day that you live.

God's Amazing Animals: Grizzlies Are Big and Tall

The average male grizzly bear is about 7 feet tall and weighs between 400 to 600 pounds. If only they could learn to play basketball, they'd be rich!

FOLLOWING IN THE FOOTSTEPS

Whoever serves me must follow me. Then my servant will be with me everywhere I am. My Father will honor anyone who serves me.

John 12:26 NCV

If you genuinely want to make choices that are pleasing to God, you must ask yourself this question: "How does God want me to serve others?"

Whatever your age, wherever you happen to be, you may be certain of this: service to others is an integral part of God's plan for your life.

Every single day of your life, including this one, God will give you opportunities to serve Him by serving other people. Welcome those opportunities with open arms. They are God's gift to you, His way of allowing you to achieve greatness in His kingdom.

The heaviest end of the cross lies ever on His shoulders. If He bids us carry a burden, He carries it also.

C. H. Spurgeon

God's Amazing Animals: A Big Baby

A blue whale baby weighs two tons at birth and gains an extra 200 pounds every day throughout its first year of life.

LIVING ABOVE THE DAILY WHINE

Do everything readily and cheerfully—no bickering, no second-guessing allowed! Go out into the world uncorrupted, a breath of fresh air in this squalid and polluted society. Provide people with a glimpse of good living and of the living God. Carry the light-giving Message into the night.

Philippians 2:14-15 MSG

Sometimes, we lose sight of our blessings. Ironically, most of us have more blessings than we can count, but we may still find reasons to complain about the minor frustrations of everyday life. To do so, of course, is not only wrong; it is also the pinnacle of shortsightedness and a serious roadblock on the path to spiritual abundance.

Are you tempted to complain about the inevitable minor frustrations of everyday living? Don't do it! Today and every day, make it a practice to count your blessings, not your hardships. It's the truly decent way to live.

God's Amazing Animals: Beware of Any Mean Moose

Although most people are more afraid of bears than moose, more people are injured each year by moose than by bears.

TRUSTING GOD'S WORD

But He answered, "It is written: Man must not live on bread alone, but on every word that comes from the mouth of God."

Matthew 4:4 HCSB

The Bible is unlike any other book. A. W. Tozer wrote, "The purpose of the Bible is to bring people to Christ, to make them holy and prepare them for heaven. In this it is unique among books, and it always fulfills its purpose."

As Christians, we are called upon to share God's Holy Word with a world in desperate need of His healing hand. The Bible is a priceless gift, a tool for Christians to use as they share the Good News of their Savior, Christ Jesus. Too many Christians, however, keep their spiritual tool kits tightly closed and out of sight.

Jonathan Edwards advised, "Be assiduous in reading the Holy Scriptures. This is the fountain whence all knowledge in divinity must be derived. Therefore let not this treasure lie by you neglected." God's Holy Word is, indeed, a priceless, one-of-a-kind treasure. Handle it with care, but more importantly, handle it every day.

Pet Facts: Smart Dogs!

Many experts believe that the border collie is the smartest dog breed.

WHAT KIND OF EXAMPLE?

You should be an example to the believers in speech, in conduct, in love, in faith, in purity.

1 Timothy 4:12 HCSB

Whether we like it or not, all of us are examples. The question is not whether we will be examples to our families and friends; the question is simply what kind of examples will we be.

What kind of example are you? Are you the kind of person whose life serves as a powerful example of righteousness? Are you a young woman whose behavior serves as a positive role model for younger folks? Are you the kind of girl whose actions, day in and day out, are honorable, ethical, and admirable? If so, you are not only blessed by God, but you are also a powerful force for good in a world that desperately needs positive influences such as yours.

D. L. Moody advised, "A person ought to live so that everybody knows he is a Christian, and most of all, his family ought to know." And that's sound advice because our families and friends are watching . . . and so, for that matter, is God.

Pet Facts: Rescued!

Over half of American adults report that they have adopted at least one rescue animal.

THE RIGHT KIND OF PEER PRESSURE

Therefore, my dear brothers, be steadfast, immovable, always abounding in the Lord's work, knowing that your labor in the Lord is not in vain.

1 Corinthians 15:58 HCSB

Some friends encourage us to obey God—these friends help us make wise choices. Other friends put us in situations where we are tempted to disobey God—these friends tempt us to make unwise choices.

Are you hanging out with people who make you a better Christian, or are you spending time with people who encourage you to stray from your faith? The answer to this question will help determine the condition of your spiritual health. One of the best ways to ensure that you follow Christ is to find fellow believers who are willing to follow Him with you.

If you choose to awaken a passion for God, you will have to choose your friends wisely.

Lisa Bevere

God's Amazing Animals: Underwater Workers

Beavers are skilled at working underwater. They use their tails to steer themselves, and they can hold their breath for 15 minutes, or more.

EVERY DAY IS A SPECIAL DAY

David and the whole house of Israel were celebrating before the Lord.

2 Samuel 6:5 HCSB

In the game of life, every day should be cause for celebration. So hopefully you feel like celebrating! After all, today (like every other day) is a gift from the Father above, so every day should be a special time to thank the Creator for all the wonderful things He has done for you and yours.

Please don't wait for birthdays or holidays; start your celebration today. Make every day a special day, including this one. Take time to pause and thank God for His gifts. He deserves your thanks, and you deserve to celebrate!

If you can forgive the person you were, accept the person you are, and believe in the person you will become, you are headed for joy. So celebrate your life.

Barbara Johnson

Pet Facts: The Brits Like Their Pets!

The British are fond of their pets. In fact, at least half of the homes in England have at least one pet. Cats and birds are British favorites.

ABOVE AND BEYOND OUR WORRIES

So don't worry about tomorrow, because tomorrow will have its own worries. Each day has enough trouble of its own.

Matthew 6:34 NCV

When we're worried, there are two places we should take our concerns: to the people who love us and to God.

When troubles arise, it helps to talk about them with parents, grandparents, concerned adults, and trusted friends. But we shouldn't stop there: we should also talk to God through our prayers.

If you're worried about something, pray about it. Remember that God is always listening, and He always wants to hear from you.

So when you're upset about something, try this simple plan: talk and pray. Talk openly to the people who love you, and pray to the Heavenly Father who made you. The more you talk and the more you pray, the better you'll feel.

God's Amazing Animals: Built-in Snowshoes

Canada lynxes, which are wild cats, have large paws that act as build-in snowshoes for walking across snow. While Canada lynxes and bobcats are similar in size, the Canada lynx's paws are almost twice as big as the bobcat's.

PRAYER: MORE IS BETTER

Rejoice always! Pray constantly. Give thanks in everything, for this is God's will for you in Christ Jesus.

1 Thessalonians 5:16-18 HCSB

Genuine, heartfelt prayer changes things and it changes us. When we lift our hearts to our Father in heaven, we open ourselves to a never-ending source of divine wisdom and infinite love.

Do you have questions that you simply can't answer? Ask for the guidance of your Father in heaven. Whatever your need, no matter how great or small, pray about it. Instead of waiting for mealtimes or bedtimes, follow the instruction of your Savior: pray always and never lose heart. And remember: God is not just near; He is here, and He's ready to talk with you. Now!

God's Amazing Animals: What's for Breakfast?

Grizzly bears usually hibernate (go into a very deep sleep) for 5 or 6 months in the winter. During that time, they don't eat anything, so they're very hungry when they wake up!

WHEN THE PATH IS DARK

Though I sit in darkness, the Lord will be my light.

Micah 7:8 HCSB

Doubts come in several shapes and sizes: doubts about God, doubts about the future, and doubts about our own abilities, for starters. But when doubts creep in, as they will from time to time, we need not despair.

God never leaves our side, not for an instant. He is always with us, always willing to calm the storms of life. When we sincerely seek His presence—and when we genuinely seek to establish a deeper, more meaningful relationship Him—God is prepared to touch our hearts, calm our fears, answer our doubts, and restore our confidence.

Ignoring Him by neglecting prayer and Bible reading will cause you to doubt.

Anne Graham Lotz

God's Amazing Animals: Polar Bears Like Water

Polar bears spend most of their time at sea because that's where they catch their food. To eat that food, they use 42 big, sharp teeth!

TRUSTING YOUR CONSCIENCE

Don't let evil get the best of you; get the best of evil by doing good.

Romans 12:21 MSG

Billy Graham correctly observed, "Most of us follow our conscience as we follow a wheelbarrow. We push it in front of us in the direction we want to go." To do so, of course, is a profound mistake. Yet all of us, on occasion, have failed to listen to the voice that God planted in our hearts, and all of us have suffered the consequences.

God gave you a conscience for a very good reason: to make your path conform to His will. Wise believers make it a practice to listen carefully to that quiet internal voice. Count yourself among that number. When your conscience speaks, listen and learn. In all likelihood, God is trying to get His message through. And in all likelihood, it is a message that you desperately need to hear.

God's Amazing Animals: Strong Legs and a Strong Back

The camel's thin legs are strong enough to carry not only its own body weight (which could be over 1,500 pounds), but also loads of cargo weighing up to 1,000 pounds.

WHEN THINGS GO WRONG

I do not consider myself yet to have taken hold of it. But one thing I do: Forgetting what is behind and straining toward what is ahead, I press on toward the goal to win the prize for which God has called me heavenward in Christ Jesus.

Philippians 3:13-14 NIV

When things don't turn out right, it's easy for most of us to give up. But usually, it's wrong. Why are we tempted to give up so quickly? Perhaps it's because we're afraid that we might embarrass ourselves if we tried hard but didn't succeed.

If you're having a little trouble getting something done, don't get mad, don't get frustrated, don't get discouraged, and don't give up. Just keep trying . . . and keep believing in yourself.

When you try hard—and keep trying hard—you can do amazing things . . . but if you quit at the first sign of trouble, you'll miss out. So here's a good rule to follow: when you have something that you want to finish, be brave enough (and wise enough) to finish it . . . you'll feel better about yourself when you do.

Pet Facts: The Favorite Insect Pet in Japan?

Many people in Japan keep crickets as pets. That's something to chirp about!

OBEY GOD AND BE HAPPY

I will praise you, Lord, with all my heart. I will tell all the miracles you have done. I will be happy because of you; God Most High, I will sing praises to your name.

Psalm 9:1-2 NCV

Do you want to be happy? Here are some things you should do: Love God and His Son, Jesus; obey the Golden Rule; and always try to do the right thing. When you do these things, you'll discover that happiness goes hand-in-hand with good behavior.

The happiest people do not behave badly; the happiest people are not cruel or greedy. The happiest people don't say unkind things. The happiest people are those who love God and follow His rules—starting, of course, with the Golden one.

Those who are God's without reserve are, in every sense, content.

Hannah Whitall Smith

Pet Facts: Why Whiskers?

Experts believe that dogs use their whiskers to help them sense the world around them. A dog's whiskers are sensitive to touch and temperature, so don't give your pet a shave!

HE IS HERE

Every morning he wakes me. He teaches me to listen like a student. The Lord God helps me learn . . . .

Isaiah 50:4-5 NCV

Do you ever wonder if God is really here? If so, you're not the first person to think such thoughts. In fact, some of the biggest heroes in the Bible had their doubts—and so, perhaps, will you. But when questions arise and doubts begin to creep into your mind, remember this: God hasn't gone on vacation; He hasn't left town; and He doesn't have an unlisted number. You can talk with Him anytime you feel like it. In fact, He's right here, right now, listening to your thoughts and prayers, watching over your every move.

Sometimes, you will allow yourself to become very busy, and that's when you may be tempted to ignore God. But, when you quiet yourself long enough to acknowledge His presence, God will touch your heart and restore your spirits. By the way, He's ready to talk right now. Are you?

God's Amazing Animals: Big Wings!

A bald eagle's wingspan can be 8 feet or more. No wonder they can fly so well!

LIVING ON PURPOSE

God chose you to be his people, so I urge you now to live the life to which God called you.

Ephesians 4:1 NCV

Life is best lived on purpose. And purpose, like everything else in the universe, begins with God. Whether you realize it or not, God has a plan for your life, a direction in which He is leading you. When you welcome God into your heart and establish a genuine relationship with Him, He will begin, in time, to make His purposes known.

Sometimes, God's intentions will be clear to you; other times, God's plan will seem uncertain at best. But even on those difficult days when you are unsure which way to turn, you must never lose sight of these overriding facts: God created you for a reason; He has important work for you to do; and He's waiting patiently for you to do it.

And the next step is up to you.

Pet Facts:
Dogs Are Becoming More Popular in China

Twenty years ago, few dogs lived Beijing, China. Today, Beijing officials say that 900,000 licensed dogs live there. And, that doesn't count the thousands of dogs that don't have a license!

HELPING THE HELPLESS

In every way I've shown you that by laboring like this, it is necessary to help the weak and to keep in mind the words of the Lord Jesus, for He said, "It is more blessed to give than to receive."

Acts 20:35 HCSB

The words of Jesus are clear: "Freely you have received, freely give" (Matthew 10:8 NIV). As followers of Christ, we are commanded to be generous with our friends, with our families, and especially with those in need. We must give freely of our time, our possessions, our love.

In 2 Corinthians 9, Paul reminds us "God loves a cheerful giver" (v. 7 NKJV). So take God's words to heart and make this pledge: Be a cheerful, generous, courageous giver. The world needs your help, and you need the spiritual rewards that will be yours when you do.

Wise Christians will be generous with their neighbors and live peaceably with them.

Warren Wiersbe

God's Amazing Animals: Chew, and Chew Some More

Beavers' front teeth never stop growing. So, beavers keep their teeth from getting too long by constantly chewing on things.

GOD WILL FORGIVE YOU

If we claim that we're free of sin, we're only fooling ourselves. A claim like that is errant nonsense. On the other hand, if we admit our sins—make a clean breast of them—he won't let us down; he'll be true to himself. He'll forgive our sins and purge us of all wrongdoing.

1 John 1:8-9 MSG

Are you perfect? Of course not! Even if you're a very good person, you're bound to make mistakes and lots of them.

When you make a mistake, you must try your best to learn from it (so that you won't make the very same mistake again). And, if you have hurt someone—or if you have disobeyed God—you must ask for forgiveness. And here's the good news: when you ask for God's forgiveness, He will always give it. God forgives you every single time you ask Him to. So ask!

God's Amazing Animals: High-Flying Eagles

Bald eagles can fly to an altitude of 10,000 feet. During level flight, they can maintain speeds of about 50 miles per hour. But, eagles can reach speeds of 100 miles per hour when they dive out of the sky!

SMALL ACTS OF KINDNESS

Whatever you did for one of the least of these brothers of Mine, you did for Me.

Matthew 25:40 HCSB

Kindness is a choice. Sometimes, when we feel happy or generous, we find it easy to be kind. Other times, when we are discouraged or tired, we can scarcely summon the energy to utter a single kind word. But, God's commandment is clear: He intends that we make the conscious choice to treat others with kindness and respect, no matter our circumstances, no matter our emotions.

In the busyness and confusion of daily life, it is easy to lose focus, and it is easy to become frustrated. We are imperfect human beings struggling to manage our lives as best we can, but we often fall short. When we are distracted or disappointed, we may neglect to share a kind word or a kind deed. This oversight hurts others, but it hurts us most of all.

Today, slow yourself down and be alert for people who need your smile, your kind words, or your helping hand. Make kindness a centerpiece of your dealings with others. They will be blessed, and you will be, too.

God's Amazing Animals: Lots of Fish Lovers

Over 12 million American families own pet fish.

FIRST THINGS FIRST

Happy is the person who finds wisdom, the one who gets understanding.

Proverbs 3:13 NCV

When something important needs to be done, the best time to do it is sooner rather than later. But sometimes, instead of doing the smart thing (which, by the way, is choosing "sooner"), we may choose "later." When we do, we may pay a heavy price for our shortsightedness.

Are you one of those people who puts things off till the last minute? If so, it's time to change your ways. Your procrastination is probably the result of your shortsighted attempt to postpone (or avoid altogether) the discomfort that you associate with a particular activity. Get over it!

Whatever "it" is, do it now. When you do, you won't have to worry about "it" later.

Pet Facts: The Chinese Love Their Cats!

In China, cats are thought to bring good luck. So the Chinese like to keep cats in their shops as well as their homes.

SPENDING TIME WITH GOD

Careful planning puts you ahead in the long run; hurry and scurry puts you further behind.

Proverbs 21:5 MSG

How much time do you spend getting to know God? A lot? A little? Almost none? Hopefully, you answered, "a lot."

God loved this world so much that He sent His Son to save it. And now only one real question remains for you: what will you do in response to God's love? God deserves your prayers, your obedience, your praise, your worship, and your love—and He deserves these things all day every day, not just on Sunday mornings.

Frustration is not the will of God. There is time to do anything and everything that God wants us to do.

Elisabeth Elliot

God's Amazing Animals: Fish with Long Lives

If properly cared for, some goldfish can outlive dogs or cats. In fact, some goldfish can live over 20 years!

THE BEST EXCUSE IS NO EXCUSE

Each of us will be rewarded for his own hard work.

1 Corinthians 3:8 TLB

Anybody can make up excuses, and you can too. But you shouldn't get into the habit of making too many excuses. Why? Because excuses don't work. And why don't they work? Because people have already heard so many excuses that most folks can recognize a phony excuse when they hear them.

So the next time you're tempted to make up an excuse, don't. Instead of making an excuse, do what you think is right. After all, the very best excuse of all . . . is no excuse.

Making up a string of excuses is usually harder than doing the work.

Marie T. Freeman

God's Amazing Animals: Eagles Are Not as Heavy as You Think

Bald eagles are big birds, with wingspans that average 6 to 8 feet. But these amazing birds are surprisingly light, weighing from 10 to 14 pounds.

IF YOU'RE TRYING TO BE PERFECT

The Lord says, "Forget what happened before, and do not think about the past. Look at the new thing I am going to do. It is already happening. Don't you see it? I will make a road in the desert and rivers in the dry land."

Isaiah 43:18-19 NCV

If you're a girl who's trying to be perfect, you're trying to do something that's impossible. No matter how much you try, you can't be a perfect person . . . and that's okay.

God doesn't expect you to live a mistake-free life—and neither should you. In the game of life, God expects you to try, but He doesn't always expect you to win. Sometimes, you'll make mistakes, but even then, you shouldn't give up!

So remember this: you don't have to be perfect to be a wonderful person. In fact, you don't even need to be "almost-perfect." You simply must try your best and leave the rest up to God.

God's Amazing Animals: Faster Than a Cheetah . . .

The peregrine falcon is the fastest animal on earth. When diving out of the sky, it can reach speeds of 200 miles per hour!

GET ENOUGH REST

Are you tired? Worn out? Burned out on religion? Come to me. Get away with me and you'll recover your life. I'll show you how to take a real rest. Walk with me and work with me…watch how I do it. Learn the unforced rhythms of grace. I won't lay anything heavy or ill-fitting on you. Keep company with me and you'll learn to live freely and lightly.

Matthew 11:28-30 MSG

Even the most inspired Christians can, from time to time, find themselves "running out of gas." If you currently fit that description, remember that God expects you to do your work, but He also intends for you to rest. When you fail to take time for sufficient rest, you do a disservice to yourself, to your family, and to your friends.

Is your energy running low? Is your spiritual tank near empty? Are your emotions frayed? If so, it's time to turn your thoughts and your prayers to God. And when you're finished, it's time to treat yourself to a heaping helping of "R&R," which stands for "Rest and Renewal."

Pet Facts: Counting Cat Teeth

An adult cat has 30 teeth: 16 on the top and 14 on the bottom.

A LIFE OF PRAYER

May the words of my mouth and the thoughts of my heart be pleasing to you, O Lord, my rock and my redeemer.

Psalm 19:14 NLT

Is prayer an integral part of your daily life, or is it a hit-or-miss habit? Do you "pray without ceasing," or is your prayer life an afterthought? Do you regularly pray in the solitude of the early morning darkness, or do you bow your head only when others are watching?

The quality of your spiritual life will be in direct proportion to the quality of your prayer life. Today, instead of turning things over in your mind, turn them over to God in prayer. Instead of worrying about your next decision, ask God to lead the way. Don't limit your prayers to the dinner table or the bedside table. Pray constantly about things great and small. God is always listening; it's up to you to do the rest.

Pet Facts: Dogs Have Been Friends for a Long Time

Throughout history, the dog has been a favorite friend to people. Dogs have also been used as workers because they're great at performing many different jobs.

PUTTING FAITH TO THE TEST

Be not afraid, only believe.

Mark 5:36 KJV

Life is a tapestry of good days and difficult days, with good days predominating. During the good days, we are tempted to take our blessings for granted (a temptation that we must resist with all our might). But, during life's difficult days, we discover precisely what we're made of. And more importantly, we discover what our faith is made of.

Has your faith been put to the test yet? If so, then you know that with God's help, you can endure life's darker days. But if you have not yet faced the inevitable trials and tragedies of life-here-on-earth, don't worry: you will. And when your faith is put to the test, rest assured that God is perfectly willing—and always ready—to give you strength for the struggle.

God's Amazing Animals: A Long Tongue Means Lots of Ants

The giant anteater's tongue is 2 feet long, which makes it easy to snack on its two favorite foods: termites and ants!

SHARING WITH YOUR FAMILY

A person who gives to others will get richer. Whoever helps others will himself be helped.

Proverbs 11:25 ICB

A good place to start sharing is at home—but it isn't always an easy place to start. Sometimes, especially when we're tired or mad, we don't treat our family members as nicely as we should. And that's too bad!

Do you have brothers and sisters? Or cousins? If so, you're lucky.

Sharing your things without whining or complaining is a wonderful way to show your family that you love them. So the next time a brother or sister or cousin asks to borrow something, say "yes" without getting mad (or feeling resentful). It's a great way to say, "I love you."

What is your focus today? Joy comes when it is Jesus first, others second . . . then you.

Kay Arthur

God's Amazing Animals: Eagles Live a Long Time

Eagles in the wild can live as long as 30 years.

THE PATH

But grow in the special favor and knowledge of our Lord and Savior Jesus Christ. To him be all glory and honor, both now and forevermore. Amen.

2 Peter 3:18 NLT

When will you be a "fully-grown" Christian? Hopefully never—or at least not until you arrive in heaven! As a believer living here on planet earth, you're never "fully grown"; you always have the potential to keep growing.

In those quiet moments when you open your heart to God, the One who made you keeps remaking you. He gives you direction, perspective, wisdom, and courage.

Would you like a time-tested formula for spiritual growth? Here it is: keep studying God's Word, keep obeying His commandments, keep praying (and listening for answers), and keep trying to live in the center of God's will. When you do, you'll never stay stuck for long. You will, instead, be a growing Christian . . . and that's precisely the kind of Christian God wants you to be.

Pet Facts: A Rodeo for Guinea Pigs?

When they play, young Guinea pigs often hop around like miniature bucking broncos!

THE WAY WE SHOULD TREAT OTHERS

The whole law is made complete in this one command: "Love your neighbor as you love yourself."

Galatians 5:14 NCV

How should we treat other people? God's Word is clear: we should treat others in the same way that we wish to be treated. This Golden Rule is easy to understand, but sometimes it can be difficult to live by.

Because we are imperfect human beings, we are, on occasion, selfish, thoughtless, or cruel. But God commands us to behave otherwise. He teaches us to rise above our own imperfections and to treat others with unselfishness and love. When we observe God's Golden Rule, we help build His kingdom here on earth. And, when we share the love of Christ, we share a priceless gift; may we share it today and every day that we live.

God's Amazing Animals: Daytime Dining or a Late-Night Snack?

Hawks, like most other birds of prey, hunt for food in the daytime, while owls search for their meals at night.

HAPPINESS IS . . .

Happy are the people who live at your Temple . . . .
Happy are those whose strength comes from you.

Psalm 84:4-5 NKJV

D o you seek happiness, abundance, and contentment? If so, here are some things you should do: Love God and His Son; depend upon God for strength; try, to the best of your abilities, to follow God's will; and strive to obey His Holy Word. When you do these things, you'll discover that happiness goes hand-in-hand with righteousness. The happiest people are not those who rebel against God; the happiest people are those who love God and obey His commandments.

What does life have in store for you? A world full of possibilities (of course it's up to you to seize them), and God's promise of abundance (of course it's up to you to accept it). So, remember to celebrate the life that God has given you. Your Creator has blessed you beyond measure. Honor Him with your prayers, your words, your deeds, and your joy.

God's Amazing Animals: Fish, Fish, and More Fish

Experts have identified over 25,000 different kinds of fish, and they believe that there may still be 15,000 kinds of fish that have not yet been identified.

CHOICES PLEASING TO GOD

If you need wisdom—if you want to know what God wants you to do—ask him, and he will gladly tell you. He will not resent your asking.

James 1:5 NLT

All of us make choices—lots of them. When we make choices that are pleasing to our Heavenly Father, we are blessed. When we make choices that cause us to walk in the footsteps of God's Son, we enjoy the abundance that Christ has promised to those who follow Him. But when we make choices that are displeasing to God, we sow seeds that have the potential to bring forth a bitter harvest.

Today, as you encounter the challenges of everyday living, you will make hundreds of choices. Choose wisely. Make your thoughts and your actions pleasing to God. And remember: every choice that is displeasing to Him is the wrong choice—no exceptions.

God's Amazing Animals: Don't Worry: An Eagle Won't Pick You Up and Fly Away

An eagle is able to lift about 4 pounds. That means it can fly away with a fish, but not you!

TOO MANY TEMPTATIONS

But remember that the temptations that come into your life are no different from what others experience. And God is faithful. He will keep the temptation from becoming so strong that you can't stand up against it. When you are tempted, he will show you a way out so that you will not give in to it.

1 Corinthians 10:13 NLT

You live in a temptation-filled world. The devil is hard at work in your neighborhood, and so are his helpers. Here in the 21st century, the bad guys are working around the clock to lead you astray. That's why you must remain vigilant.

In a letter to believers, Peter offers a stern warning: "Your adversary, the devil, prowls around like a roaring lion, seeking someone to devour" (1 Peter 5:8 NASB). What was true in New Testament times is equally true in our own. Satan tempts his prey and then devours them (and it's up to you—and only you—to make sure that you're not one of the ones being devoured!).

As a person who seeks a life-changing relationship with Jesus, you must beware because temptations are everywhere. Satan is determined to win; you must be equally determined that he does not.

God's Amazing Animals: Time for School

A group of fish is called a "school."

A CHANGE OF HEART

The one who conceals his sins will not prosper, but whoever confesses and renounces them will find mercy.

Proverbs 28:13 HCSB

Who among us has sinned? All of us. But, God calls upon us to turn away from sin by following His commandments. And the good news is this: When we do ask God's forgiveness and turn our hearts to Him, He forgives us absolutely and completely.

Genuine repentance requires more than simply offering God apologies for the things we've done wrong. Real repentance may start with apologies to God, but it ends only when we turn away from the sins that distance us from Him. In truth, we offer our most meaningful apologies to God not with our words, but with our actions. As long as we are still engaged in sin, we may be "repenting," but we have not fully "repented."

God's Amazing Animals: The Biggest Penguin

The emperor penguin is the tallest kind of penguin. It can grow to be almost 4 feet tall.

SHARING THE GOOD NEWS

Go therefore and make disciples of all the nations, baptizing them in the name of the Father and of the Son and of the Holy Spirit, teaching them to observe all things that I have commanded you; and lo, I am with you always, even to the end of the age.

Matthew 28:19-20 NKJV

After His resurrection, Jesus addressed His disciples. As recorded in the 28th chapter of Matthew, Christ instructed His followers to share His message with the world. This "Great Commission" applies to Christians of every generation, including our own.

As believers, we are called to share the Good News of Jesus with our families, with our neighbors, and with the world. Christ commanded His disciples to become fishers of men. We must do likewise, and we must do so today. Tomorrow may indeed be too late.

God's Amazing Animals:
Don't Try to Catch This One with a Cane Pole!

The biggest fish in the world is the whale shark, which can reach fifty feet in length.

GOD IS LOVE

We know how much God loves us, and we have put our trust in him. God is love, and all who live in love live in God, and God lives in them.

1 John 4:16 NLT

St. Augustine observed, "God loves each of us as if there were only one of us." Do you believe those words? Do you seek to have an intimate, one-on-one relationship with your Heavenly Father, or are you satisfied to keep Him at a "safe" distance?

Sometimes, in the crush of our daily duties, God may seem far away, but He is not. God is everywhere we have ever been and everywhere we will ever go. He is with us night and day; He knows our thoughts and our prayers. And, when we earnestly seek Him, we will find Him because He is here, waiting patiently for us to reach out to Him.

Let us reach out to Him today and always. And let us praise Him for the glorious gifts that have transformed us today and forever. Amen.

God's Amazing Animals: America's Bird

The bald eagle became America's national emblem in 1782 when the great seal of the United States was adopted.

MY FAVORITE VERSES AND
FUN ANIMAL FACTS

MY FAVORITE VERSES AND
FUN ANIMAL FACTS

MY FAVORITE VERSES AND FUN ANIMAL FACTS

MY FAVORITE VERSES AND
FUN ANIMAL FACTS

_____

_____

_____

_____

_____

_____

_____

_____

_____

_____

_____

_____

_____

_____

MY FAVORITE VERSES AND
FUN ANIMAL FACTS

_____

_____

_____

_____

_____

_____

_____

_____

_____

_____

_____

_____

_____

_____

_____

_____

MY FAVORITE VERSES AND FUN ANIMAL FACTS

_____

_____

_____

_____

_____

_____

_____

_____

_____

_____

_____

_____

_____

_____

_____

MY FAVORITE VERSES AND
FUN ANIMAL FACTS

MY FAVORITE VERSES AND FUN ANIMAL FACTS

_____

_____

_____

_____

_____

_____

_____

_____

_____

_____

_____

_____

_____

_____

_____

_____

_____

_____

MY FAVORITE VERSES AND
FUN ANIMAL FACTS

_____

_____

_____

_____

_____

_____

_____

_____

_____

_____

_____

_____

_____

_____

_____

MY FAVORITE VERSES AND
FUN ANIMAL FACTS

_____

_____

_____

_____

_____

_____

_____

_____

_____

_____

_____

_____

_____

_____

_____

_____

_____

_____

MY FAVORITE VERSES AND
FUN ANIMAL FACTS